The Power Technique of Radio-TV Copywriting

By Neil Terrell

TAB BOOKS
Blue Ridge Summit, Pa. 17214

Preface

The material in this book was written and offered originally as The POWER TECHNIQUE Radio Copywriting Course. Minor changes and additions have been made to the correspondence course material, making it suitable for reading in book form.

As you read it, you will find that it is directed to three types of working radio and TV station personnel: the beginning copywriter with no experience or training, the experienced copywriter who has had no formal study or training in advertising principles, and station salesmen (including managers) who can use much of the advertising knowledge presented here to help clients plan more effective campaigns.

While the language is directed to the copywriter, the principles and illustrations can be valuable to anyone concerned with advertising. Various illustrations of copy types written by the author are intentionally kept simple for easy analysis and understanding. More complex examples of the copywriter's art are taken from the work of several helpful and cooperative broadcasters.

Special recognition and thanks are due Si Willing, President, KMAR, Winnsboro, La., and KNNN, Friona, Tex., for his encouragement and help. Without his whole-hearted assistance this book would not have been published.

The vision, the enthusiasm expressed regarding the first two chapters, and the cooperation of Charles W. Brewer, general manager, WHIN, Gallatin, Tennessee, were instrumental in shaping parts of this work.

Lou Nelson, Flanders, N. J., staff copywriter, air personality, "spec tape" specialist, and free-lance producer, who has added to the quality of copywriting and record shows on such stations as WBUD, Trenton, and WNJR, Newark, kindly contributed samples of his work.

Paul Garrison, formerly owner of an advertising agency in Nashville, now one of the principles of International Printing & Mailing Corp. in the same city, was exceptionally helpful in opening his radio copy file. In this book you'll see some of the most effective and best known local advertising ever created in Nashville, a city noted for some of the finest radio advertising in the world.

As a copywriter you have an opportunity to occupy a unique position in your community. Your community may be a town of 2,500 or a metropolis of half a million. Whatever its size, you are either the lone professional copywriter or you're one of a very few. All the professional copywriters in a market of 100,000 could hold a convention in a Volkswagen. As a member of that select fraternity you are exerting a significant influence on the buying behavior of vast numbers of people in your market. The more effective your copy, the greater effect you have on their behavior.

The power of broadcast advertising copy to fire the imagination of vast numbers of people has resulted in FCC restrictions on the uses of it. In 1938, for instance, a dramatic show produced by Orson Welles convinced millions of people coast-to-coast, who tuned in late, that our world was being invaded by Martians. There was panic in the land for hours. The FCC ruled that such power to move men's minds was too dangerous and must not be used in that manner again.

In the 1950s, treasure hunts and similar promotions brought out crowds of excited people who mobbed downtown areas doing such things as measuring the exact width of a main intersection or following a succession of clues hidden in sidewalk gratings and behind loose bricks in downtown alleys. The FCC ruled that radio's power to move mobs of people to that particular kind of action must be shackled.

As a copywriter, you have some responsibility to use your massive power to **move the public mind** carefully and in a constructive manner. You also have a responsibility to use your ability as **powerfully** as possible to the end of moving your listeners to want the service and merchandise of your advertisers. While much of the material may appear to be directed to radio, the principles apply to TV in every respect. The difference, of course, is that the TV copywriter must keep in mind the visual effects as he plans his approach.

Lou Nelson wrapped it up like this: "Since everything is relative, copywriters can be likened to surgeons and garbage collectors. There are the great ones, the mediocre, and those who are just passing through. Talent, desire, and conviction make the great ones. One of those ingredients cannot stand by itself. A combination of all three must be used to make the potential become a reality."

Toward that end this book is directed.

Neil Terrell
Nashville, Tenn.

Contents

Chapter 1

Your Power to Persuade Listeners

The number one principle in writing effective advertising copy is what the professors like to call "the YOU attitude." That means the copywriter must write about "YOU" the listener, rather than about "me," "we," or "he" the advertiser. Less erudite but immensely practical copywriters have translated the professional YOU attitude to the "horse" principle.

A successful, long-ago copywriter explained it like this: "My horse disappeared. I asked myself, if I were a horse, where would I go. I decided that if I were a horse I would go down to the corner of the south forty, have a drink from the creek and loaf in the shade of the trees. I went there and found my horse."

He looked at the situation from the viewpoint of the horse. You must look at your copywriting problems from the viewpoint of your client's prospects.

In your imagination you must stand as close to your client's prospects as you can. Try to see the advertised product or business through your listeners' eyes—not through the eyes of the advertiser, the salesman or the client's mother-in-law!

ADVERTISER MOTIVATION

The prospect for your client's merchandise has only one reason to buy. That reason is a belief that the product or service will in some way be useful to him. The traditional explanation in sales managers' language is this: "He must expect to receive some benefit from owning or using it."

Benefits are many and widely varied.

To be effective you must constantly keep in mind the attitudes and motivations of listeners, which are quite different from those of the advertiser. The advertiser wants to sell his service or merchandise to anyone who will buy. He has no other real motivation for advertising. He will sell to anyone who is willing to buy for whatever reason.

CUSTOMER MOTIVATION

The motivation of customers is more complex. Customers buy for many reasons. Many times they, themselves, don't realize why they're buying a particular item or a specific brand. Their motivations are often complex, obscure, and based on pure emotion, while they give themselves (and others) logical-sounding rationalizations.

For instance, in buying automobiles it is obvious that most men prefer the most powerful model they can afford.

Why?

There is no rational need for any passenger car to have a 400-horsepower engine. An engine with less than half that much power is more than enough to break every speed law in the United States, with reserve power to spare.

Without defining the yearning for power in psychologists' terms, it is sufficient to say that power has a strong appeal for modern man. Some men simply acquire greater power at every opportunity in the same automatic way they choose a steak over a hamburger, with no conscious consideration of why more power is desirable. The desirability of more power is so obvious to them that they could not explain it if asked. More power is desirable; therefore, they buy the highest power available. Simple!

Others, who do think about it, realize that power has become ridiculous. Yet, they still want power simply because it is available. These men rationalize their desire for more power by saying, or believing, that it's safer to have a margin of power for passing, for getting out of, or staying out of dangerous traffic situations. A study of new car advertising since 1949 reveals all this and much more about illogical reasons for buying.

Research has determined that the strongest appeals in automobile advertising are size and luxury. The standard car salesman's pitch of "the closest trade in town" ranks way down the priority list of buying motivations. To the dealer and salesman, of course, it seems by far the best appeal because (as a result of the auto dealers' own cut-throat activities) prospective customers are prone to chisel on price to the immediate exclusion of other considerations. But the price chiseling begins only after the desirability of a particular brand or model has been established, and after the prospect has been given some reason to believe that it may be desirable to trade with that particular dealer.

As a practical matter, the copywriter at the station level sometimes must write motivational garbage to satisfy a client. Such garbage sometimes produces spectacular results simply because it is written and delivered with such imagination and enthusiasm that listeners are inspired to go and see what the excitement is about.

In most cases, garbage on the air is like garbage in the kitchen—a smelly nuisance that has no practical value. Your copy must motivate listeners to want! As a copywriter, it is your job to motivate the listener to want! It is the client's job to sell the merchandise after you send the prospects to him.

In writing automobile copy you are a more effective motivator when you hammer on the **benefits** of size and luxury, plus the **benefits** of doing business with Fred's Fine Fords (as opposed to the possibility of dealing with other Ford agencies in the area). All this is the essence of the YOU attitude.

To say it another way, **make 'em want it!** Make your prospect want what you're selling. That is the essence of any persuasive function. A criminal lawyer attempts to persuade the jury that it wants to find his client innocent. A good auto salesman is constantly trying to persuade his prospects that they want the car he's showing.

It was that great salesman, Frank Bettger, who said that when you once convince a man that he wants what you're selling, he'll twist your arm, if necessary, to get it.

As a good copywriter you should be concerned with explaining why your listener wants the car, the dress, the bank service, or whatever you're selling for your client. He wants it because of what it will do for him. A bank loan will enable him to take that Bahamas vacation he wants; a new dress, slim, sleek and lovely, will "invite compliments"; a new car will make him feel like a more powerful man in many ways.

Some of the most effective selling ever done on network radio was in noncommercial scripts read by the announcer on Jack Bailey's Queen for a Day, carried for years on MBS. The writer simply painted the listener into a beautiful picture of incredible luxury and enjoyment.

A typical script went something like this: "When you're our queen, you'll enjoy two weeks at the luxurious Seabubble resort in the beautiful Bahama Islands; you'll be flown there in the lap of luxury by Trans World Airlines; Joe Bloe, mayor of the exotic village of Seabubble, will greet you as you step off the plane amid showers of flowers. You'll live in a magnificent 6-room suite, your every need attended by two maids and a butler wearing colorful uniforms that could be straight from the gracious days of Gone With the Wind. You'll be a dinner guest at the fabulous Black Rock Restaurant, and you'll have cocktails at the world-famous Seahorse Tavern where 16 members of the exciting and never-to-be-forgotten steel band will serenade you with a song written especially for you..."

The objective was to paint a beautiful picture of the benefits enjoyed by the winning contestant, thereby motivating every woman listening to want to be Queen for a Day and enjoy the same once-in-a-lifetime thrills.

In explaining why your listener wants, many times you must be quite indirect because your listener buys for reasons that often do not conform to any obvious logic. The Queen for a Day contestant was straining every nerve with desire to win that fabulous trip to Seabubble. But was it Seabubble she really wanted? No! What she wanted was the thrill of winning. She would have been just as happy winning a trip to New York, New Orleans, Dallas, or Acapulco. She would have been happy to have won a pair of tickets to Disneyland, or hamburgers for two at McDonald's drive-in hamburger heaven in beautiful downtown Burbank.

The same psychology applies to a service or merchandise she may consider. Visualize the lady of the house. She's dressed for downtown and she's on the way, driving the family car with its white sidewalls, factory air, deep pile carpet, power windows, power ashtrays, and AM-FM radio.

The radio is turned on and she's listening to her favorite station as she anticipates several hours of shopping for a new living room suite. Deep in her own thoughts of a revitalized and sparkling new living room decor, she responds to the word "furniture" coming from the radio. It's a pleasant voice painting a picture—a beautiful picture—of distinctively handsome living room furniture, furniture that will impress the neighbors, the in-laws, and her husband's business associates with a look of tasteful affluence.

She listens: It's tastefully modern with hand-rubbed walnut trim, and comes in a wide choice of decorator colors. Besides that, it's new. Furthermore, it's on display now at a respected store, and terms are easy.

How can she resist. She did have something of a more traditional nature in mind, but this sounds so good she believes she might like it better. Like the Queen contestant who would be happy with any trip the copywriter described so beautifully, the average or typical lady of the house will be happy with any furniture that is as good as the copywriter's word picture of it.

Our lady of the house does not need furniture because she needs a suitable place for her family and friends to sit.

No!

She has furniture, relatively good furniture. Certainly it's comfortable furniture. Her need is not for furniture at all—in the physical sense. The object of her search is something to fill an emotional need. She might, indeed, fill that need with a wall-to-wall drape on one side of the room and a massive decorator clock on the other if an enterprising salesman pointed out the advantages of that arrangement. Then she might have her present furniture cleaned or recovered.

The result would be a drastically different appearance of her living room, impressing friends, neighbors, and her husband's associates with her exceptionally fine taste and with her husband's ability to provide the financing for her standards of decor.

Whether she selects a clock and drapery or a complete new suite, her reasoning appears totally illogical when viewed from the standpoint of need. It is not illogical—in fact, it is perfectly sensible—when viewed in the light of emotional need.

Emotional need is the motivation that sells furniture in this situation; and emotional need sells most other merchandise, including office equipment and industrial machinery.

The automobile buyer, like a sheep rushing into the slaughterhouse, gladly pays a higher price for surplus power he can't possibly use for any rational purpose. It does, however, serve the purpose of satisfying his emotional need to feel more powerful.

Hertz capitalized on that appeal with the slogan "we'll put YOU in the driver's seat."

Since automobile dealers are the biggest users of local radio advertising, it is well for a station copywriter to stay abreast of automobile selling philosophy.

As a general rule, the Radio Advertising Bureau has recommended that 50 percent of a retail business' advertising budget be allocated to radio. Many automobile dealers have found it profitable to devote more to radio. Some have gone as high as 80 percent.

RECOGNIZE TRENDS

The trend in automobile merchandising has been moving in two directions: toward bigger, more luxurious cars, and toward smaller, less expensive cars. But the demand for smaller, compact cars has become a trend within a trend. In Detroit the automobile game has one name: profit. That is good. No profit, no automobiles. Consequently, new rules have developed recently.

Newer, smaller, and less expensive cars have reduced the unit profit. Newer, bigger, and more expensive ideas are increasing the price and the profit on smaller cars. Detroit's merchandisers are appealing with increasing success to small-car prospects who want their small, inexpensive status symbol to say for them: "Look, my small, inexpensive car is bigger and more expensive than your small, inexpensive car."

The September 1969 issues of both **Esquire** and **True**—certainly not a coincidence—featured articles detailing the current automotive revolution. And it is a revolution. Both stories heralded the beginning of a significant change in the philosophy of the automobile, a philosophy that should be understood by every station copywriter, salesman, and manager.

Performance is the word, and the word is God. Referred to as "supercars" or "muscle cars" the hood-scooped, fat-tired, souped-up, big-braked, paint-striped performance cars are having an effect on all cars rolling off Detroit's assembly lines.

Vance Packard and Ralph Nader notwithstanding, the day of the racing start from stop lights is here. And so is the car designed especially for that activity. To hold his own in the company of 30-mile-an-hour street racing, the young swinger of today and tomorrow must have a Plymouth Road Runner, Ford Torino or Cobra, Chevelle SST 396, Dodge Charger R-T or one of the 31 other super choices.

Daniel A. Jedlicka, auto editor of the Chicago **Sun-Times**, predicts that as the young men become older and more responsive to wives' tastes in transportation, designs will be tamer for the then older buyers, but performance will remain a part of their lives.

Recognize the performance revolution. Knowledge of it will be necessary if you are to write effective automobile dealer copy from now on.

THE SIX POWER APPEALS

Psychologists have isolated six basic appeals to human nature. In elementary school you learned that the three essentials to human existence are Food, Clothing, and Shelter. Those three factors are insufficient to sustain a human being in any satisfactory mental condition. Man is a social animal and consequently has strong and definite needs of a social nature.

The list of six **Power** appeals is based on social needs and assumes that food, clothing and shelter exist as a foundation of civilized society. Here are the six **Power** appeals:

1. Happiness   4. Wealth

2. Sex   5. Esteem

3. Health   6. Security

Learn these appeals. Etch them into your brain. Know them as well as you know that Monday comes after Sunday and that two and two add up to four. These six **Power** appeals constitute the foundation of any successful copywriting effort.

Your listeners—your client's prospects—are motivated in nearly every purchase by one or more of these six considerations. Learn which appeal or combination of appeals is usually most effective for each client or type of merchandise or service you write about.

Of course, we must realize that some specific appeals are usually most effective, not always. Psychology is not an exact science. No person can ever know, with certainty, exactly what another person is thinking or feeling. No appeal is 100 percent effective. But it is a certainty that the reaction of large groups of people can be predicted.

When the ball park is packed for the last game of the world series and the home team batter clobbers the ball for a home run, it is possible to predict with absolute certainty that the crowd will bound to its collective feet and give out an exuberant roar. There may be some individual spectators who do not rise and roar with happiness. But, surely, they will be so few as to be virtually unnoticed.

Consequently, it can be predicted that a soap which promises to give the user a beauty bath as she performs the traditional drudgery of washing dishes will outsell a soap that is just as efficient but promises only to get the dishes clean.

It also can be predicted that:

—a brassiere offering a more alluring shape will outsell one that promises mere quality construction and durability.

—jewelry offering "a more glamorous you" will outsell jewelry guaranteeing merely the finest craftmanship and beauty of design.

—a house offering a desirable address in the heart of the wealthiest suburb will be desired more strongly than one that offers the finest construction, landscaping, and convenience in a less glamorous area.

—furniture offering an opportunity to live in "the charm and gracious atmosphere originated by the illustrious founders of historic Early American colonies" will far outsell furniture offering mere beauty and suitability for today's environment. (Don't be misled by this: a contemporary furniture fancier is part of an altogether different market; she wouldn't be caught dead drunk with a four-poster bed or a French provincial sofa.)

—an air conditioner that "keeps your home sealed" against dirt and various other contaminating factors will outsell the same quality machine that promises merely to keep your house cool and comfortable.

—ice cream described as a "heaping dish of creamy goodness" will outsell the same ice cream described as being jammed full of vitamin C and other untastable things that are "good for you."

—toys offering the opportunity to "enjoy watching your child learn" will outsell a simple and less expensive toy that merely promises to let your child have fun.

—a line of shoes promising "lovelier feet" will outsell a far better value that promises only "fine shoes."

BECOMING A PRO

The dabbler or the amateur thinks copy is good or bad; a pro knows it's good or bad—and why. When you learn the principles you're going to get from this book, you'll know whether copy is good, mediocre, or lousy. And you'll know why.

Learn the principles, and the techniques of using them, to increase your client's sales and you'll be a pro. Your writing ability and your vocabulary may not delight the heart of a college English teacher. But no matter. Your purpose is to motivate customers, not buck for an "A." Learn to use, effectively, the principles in this book and you'll be a pro.

The line "Winston tastes good, like a cigarette should" would bring a slashing red-pencil mark from any English teacher, yet it was the key line in one of the most successful radio and TV commercials ever written. The objective of advertising copy is to motivate. If it can be done best by violating a rule of grammar, so be it.

You'll be a pro when you're directing your copy as straight as a rifle shot to your prospects' wants rather than merely informing them. You'll be making them "want it." But you cannot hope to become an effective pro simply by reading through this book. You must get what is in it out of it—and into your mind so you can use it quickly and automatically.

Remember, always, that your job is to relate goods or services to human needs and wants. Impress that on your mind now. Etch it into your brain. Remember it always.

Relate Goods and Services To Human Needs and Wants!

To do that intelligently and efficiently you must know and remember another principle. This principle is the basis of all professional copywriting and selling. For proper emphasis it should be seen in brilliant red neon letters two feet high. Since that is impossible, you must visualize it as though it were. Read it. Think about it. Remember it. **Always!** Every day of your life.

Accept the World as it is!

Your job as a professional copywriter is to relate goods or services to human needs and wants. To do that realistically and efficiently you must know and remember to accept the world as it is, not as idealists say it is. This means that you must accept the fact that the moving force of everyone is self-love. Accept the psychologically proven fact that everything a person does is for the purpose of gratifying himself.

It is widely agreed among psychologists that every noninstinctive action we take is for the purpose of gaining approval or avoiding disapproval. Translated into practical copywriting know-how, that means your listeners buy for what they think they'll get. You tell your listeners that a Playtex padded bra "adds shape, not inches" and they immediately see how to gain the approval of appearance and avoid the disapproval of cheating.

Tell a car-proud man that the typical PennZoil customer owns fine fishing tackle and hunting guns that he's proud of, and that he is likely to be seen polishing his car on a good day because he's proud of it, and you're likely to sell some Penn-Zoil to a car-proud man. He visualizes himself sharing in the almost universal esteem accorded a man who takes excellent care of fine possessions.

Tell a housewife that Colonial Bread is "eight hours better because we give it time to be better," and you short-circuit logic with a complex emotional appeal that only depth research could explain. It strikes the same type of emotion as the "gracious atmosphere of Early American furniture." It is effective with the type of buyer whose tastes and opinions are based on a reverence for historical "charm" and tradition, regardless of facts.

Tell career girls that the private employment agency is not a matchmaker, but "who knows who you'll meet on a new job," and you start some career girls thinking about changing jobs.

Tell your bargain basement customers that while they're saving up to 30 and 40 percent, they're getting an exact copy of the style that Liz or Jackie wore in London last week and you'll start a stampede. (They feel that some of the massive jet-set approval may rub off on them.)

Describe a tube with armholes as a "delightful new style, free and fanciful, flattering to your figure and as smart as tomorrow" and you may start a new fad. Your listener will view the shapeless tube through the framework you have created and will indeed see a delightful new style. She may never understand exactly how it flatters a figure, but if you tell her it does, and keep telling her, and she sees an international gadfly, whose figure flatterability is minimal, wearing something similar on TV or in a news picture, she will be forever convinced that the tube enhances her own size 42 figure.

All these examples have one thing in common: they promise the listener more than the mere physical merchandise:

The bra buyer is promised shape.

The PennZoil buyer is promised a share of almost universal esteem.

The bread buyer is promised an unnamed and undescribed benefit based on the traditional eight hours rising time. (To the majority of listeners, tradition is like flags and motherhood—it's automatically good.)

Career girls are promised new hunting grounds.

Bargain basement dress customers are promised jet-set glamour.

Regular price dress customers are promised figure flattery, as well as fancy freedom and a head start on tomorrow's fashions.

THE POWER FORMULA

Copywriters, over the years, have evolved a formula for producing copy that is consistently powerful and that affects the sensibilities of prospects with predictable results. It has been tried and proven over many years and no better method of organizing copy appeals has been found.

It's generally referred to as the AIDA formula. The name comes from the acronym, the initial letters of the words. In one easily comprehensible form it looks like this:

A ttention

I nterest

D esire

A ction

The basic elements of the copy normally must come in that order for the most power.

Another fundamental rule of advertising that will be important to you later is this:

EVERY SO-CALLED RULE OF ADVERTISING HAS

BEEN BROKEN WITH SPECTACULAR SUCCESS

Advertising is an art. It is subject to the artistic judgment of the practitioner. Some times an astute copywriter can break rules with great success. But such successes are rare. Such success is identical to the success achieved by great cartoonists. A cartoonist must spend years learning to be a good artist before he can successfully distort his art. He must know how to do it right before he can succeed in doing it wrong correctly. He must know which rules he is breaking and why. He must know what he would accomplish by adhering to a particular rule and what he can accomplish by violating the rule. Then he must weigh one against the other to arrive at an intelligent decision.

As a radio copywriter you will have more consistent success in using the basic AIDA formula because there is proven power in that formula. In breaking the rules and departing from the well-marked path charted by the advertising geniuses who brought Listerine and Pepsodent, Texise and Arthur Murray's Dancing Schools from obscurity to top sellers, you venture into unknown territory. Out in that vast, uncharted wilderness, very little, if anything, has been proven. Little is known about results that might stem from a distortion of the formula. One important fact that is known is this: **The odds are against it.**

To a casual listener it may seem that many national radio commercials depart from the basic formula. But closer analysis usually reveals that, while they are done with considerable cleverness, they are built on the proven power foundation—the AIDA formula. Throughout this book we will be concerned with the basic formula. Successful "cartooning" of your copy can come only from your own imagination.

Attention

Certainly the element that attracts attention must be first; otherwise, the remainder of the copy will be largely wasted. There are many ways to get the attention of your listeners. In these days of easily produced recorded commercials, a sound effect is helpful in many cases. A statement, a question, a promise of a benefit, or a bit of the right kind of news will get attention.

Interest and Desire

It is almost equally obvious that before we logically can ask the prospect to buy, we must first arouse his interest in and his desire for the product or service. Some ways to do this are:

1. Immediately enlarge on your attention-compelling lead.

2. Emphasize one basic area.

3. Tell about the benefits of owning or using it.

4. Tell selling points that will deliver those benefits.

5. Show that it is easy, economical, enjoyable.

6. Use the appeal of sex and-or prestige if you can.

7. Use negative inferences; show ills avoided by using it. (Notice that this has lowest priority; better techniques usually can be found.)

Urge to Action

Usually, it is best to close with an urge to action: Get it today. Look for the big red label when you're in the supermarket. Ask for PennZoil next time you need a quart. Shop Smart's Celebration Sale and Save.

You pack more power into your urge to action when you set the stage for it logically. (Remember that it's the customers who are illogical. You must be coldly logical about your copy appeals.) Usually, you should save your strongest appeal to use immediately preceding your urge to action. Here are some reasons that have been effective in some of the best advertising produced.

1. Good reasons and excuses for buying.

2. Make selection—or buying—easy.

3. Tell how, when, and where to get it.

4. Give prices and terms—make it easy.

5. Make it sell for this client alone. Don't let competitors get a free ride, thereby diluting results.

6. Sell now as the time to buy.

There are other ways to pack people-moving power into your copy by using strategems that add distinction to your offering and to create conviction. Those listed here, along with others, will be discussed and analyzed in detail.

SUMMARY

1. Ability to write effective copy is the power to move mens' minds.

2. You must use the YOU attitude rather than the "me," "we," or "he" attitude.

3. Customers don't always understand the reasons they buy.

4. The most desirable features in automobiles are size and luxury.

5. It is often helpful to paint a beautiful picture of your prospect enjoying the benefits of the product or service.

6. Consumer buying is based mostly on emotional needs rather than physical needs.

7. The six **Power** appeals are:

1. Happiness	4. Wealth
2. Sex	5. Esteem
3. Health	6. Security

8. All buying is done for one or more of these reasons.

9. The response of masses of people to specific ideas is fairly predictable.

10. Copy that **sells** is copy that offers **more** than the physical merchandise.

11. You must **always** relate goods and services to human needs and wants.

12. You must accept the fact that self-love is the basis for buying.

13. While the rules of copywriting are sometimes successfully broken, it is best to stick to the AIDA formula.

14. The first element of copy is the attention compeller.

15. Next, it is necessary to arouse interest and create desire.

16. The final element in copy is the urge to action.

Chapter 2

Develop Your Maximum Power

Analyze your client's various appeals to find the maximum power. The first step is to find the answer to this question:

What is the greatest benefit your listener would receive from buying?

It would seem to have an immediately obvious answer, but that is not always the case. Research has revealed that hidden motivations exert tremendous influence on decisions to buy. Hidden motivations are based purely on **emotion** rather than on any logical benefits that may result from owning or using the product or service.

One example of a hidden motivation used during the summer of 1969 was the campaign for Sealtest's Light and Lively ice milk. Twice in each commercial the point was made that, because of a reduction in calories without sacrificing the richness of taste, you can eat twice as much "if you want to."

The obvious benefits of ice cream are delicious taste and enjoyment. But motivational research has revealed that ice cream has an emotional tie to childhood. The enjoyment of ice cream is associated with the emotions stemming from childhood experiences relating to huge, heaping, running-over dishes of ice cream. Not just plenty of ice cream, but a super abundance of ice cream. Consequently, the repeated suggestion that "you can eat twice as much if you want to" without taking on a super abundance of calories was effective in moving large numbers of people to buy Light and Lively ice milk.

Another example of a hidden (but not very well) motivation in action was a series of radio commercials used by Dealy-Rourke employment agency in Nashville. Using drive-time spots and newscasts, as career girls were on their way home (perhaps sick of their present jobs with irritable, hard-to-please bosses), the agency sometimes made a back-handed pitch for romance.

Theme of this copy was: "Dealy-Rourke is a career-maker, not a match-maker; but who knows what kind of dreamy man, with a sports car and boat, you'll meet if you change jobs."

An illogical, purely emotional block motivates many people to avoid Minnie Pearl's fried chicken and roast beef restaurants. The block stems from the basic motivation of pride which can be identified as snobbery. They have a prideful aversion to anything connected with country music, The Grand Ol' Opry, and down-to-earth unsophisticated rural honesty. Consequently, they refuse to be seen patronizing a restaurant bearing the name of a star whose audiences for 25 years have been of a mostly unsophisticated type.

Noble-Dury agency attempted to overcome that block in relation to Minnie Pearl's roast beef restaurants. Commercials were done by a stuffed-shirt type British voice expressing amazement that "Minnie Pearl has really done it" with fine roast beef.

Two implications were not at all hidden from the audience at which they were aimed:

A. Minnie's roast beef is good enough for British nobility.

B. The nobility is concerned only with the fine quality of the roast beef.

A chain of Mahalia Jackson's fast food restaurants was faced with the same type of motivations—good and bad. Her name is enough to attract many customers—black and white. Her name, also, seems likely to demotivate not only a substantial number of potential white customers but many of the fast-growing Negro upper middle class group. The motivation is pride, the same factor affecting Minnie's business.

Such demotivating factors are food for much professional cogitating. They call for complex thought and careful planning. But the end result of the campaign was to sell:

A. Good food

B. The desirability of going to Mahalia's for good food.

Thus it is in all advertising copy. You must point out the benefits of buying or using. Sometimes the tree of benefits is difficult to see in the forest of objections.

What other benefits would your listener receive from buying?

Ask yourself—or your client—what secondary benefits are inherent in the product or service. In the case of Minnie

Pearl's restaurants, there is a desire on the part of many customers merely to enter Minnie's premises because of the aura surrounding a great star of country music, and more lately, network TV.

Assuming for the moment that this is the **Power** appeal, what, then, are the secondary appeals? Copy certainly should include these appeals:

A. Convenient location

B. Plenty of parking space

C. Fast service

D. Take it out or eat it there

E. Quality food

In planning your copy appeals, look for traits that suggest:

A. Enjoyment

B. Convenience

C. Quality

D. Value (durability, size, superior features, beauty)

E. Snobbery

F. Safety

G. Appetite

H. Relation to any of the five senses

In Chapter 12 you'll find an analysis of many different types of products and businesses from the viewpoint of buying motivations. It will be helpful to check for hidden or illogical motivations in writing copy for any product or service.

Check national advertising.

In the case of nationally advertised products such as automobiles, clothing, food, appliances, branded building materials, boats, some clothing, etc., which are also advertised by retailers, a review of the manufacturer's national advertising in magazines, newspapers, TV and brochures can point out buying motivations for you.

For instance, in 1969 Buick called itself "a heavy car; a luxurious car; the ideal car for a cowboy with a family."

A tie-in with the national motivating appeals and ideas will give your local client the benefit of massive momentum already built up by the manufacturer. Your listeners have, of course, been exposed to that national advertising on radio, TV, in magazines, newspapers, and perhaps billboards, or even book matches. Such a tie-in is beneficial in two ways:

A. It gives your client the benefit of extensive and expensive research and testing that has indicated the strongest appeals.

B. It gives your client the benefit of perhaps millions of dollars already invested by the manufacturer in promoting those appeals.

In this connection, Joseph Stone, president, Berger, Stone & Partners, Inc., a New York advertising agency, offers this advice: "If he's the area's only dealer of his make of car, he's wise to push the brand. But, if he competes with many nearby dealers of the same car, he must, to a greater degree, say, 'Buy it here ...and here's why!' But mere generalities won't do it. He has to give specific 'Why-me' reasons, such as: handier location, easier parking, friendlier service and warranty work, more mechanics, better facilities, bigger parts stock, greater trade-in allowances because of his huge used car business, better credit terms, etc."

Most new ideas are accepted only after the sixth impression, according to a research report from the Psychology Department of the University of Texas. This means that if the manufacturer has borne the cost of making six or more impressions of his current motivational ploy on the minds of your listeners, your use of the same attack on their resistance will be more successful than if you make the first impression of a different reason to buy.

Suppose you're writing copy for a used car dealer who is promoting a 1969 Buick. One of the most effective things you can do to arouse desire for that Buick is to use the same appeal that Buick is using every day. Tell your local listeners that "this is a heavy car; a luxurious car."

While the cowboy connection may be too far out in your market, you might find a similar appeal that does fit your market. The cowboy is, of course, used to create an image of the Buick as associated with rough, tough, active he-men, but also ideal for the wives and families of those same he-men. If you're serious about producing great advertising for your local dealer in this hypothetical situation, then you might consider an association with the image of a locally respected type: entertainers, stock car drivers, jockey, yacht racer, professional athlete, etc. This type of thinking could lead to an extensive campaign for a client who deals in automobiles, boats, or lawn mowers.

Review your own knowledge of the product, service, or store.

You, as an alert member of a progressive-minded business staff, are aware of many facts accumulated casually and unconsciously. Much of your tremendous store of knowledge can serve a useful function in copywriting by a simple review of what you may already know about your client or his products.

Although you may have been handed a scribbled list of "specials" with no motivating information except price, you know, for instance, that bell-bottom slacks are "in." You know that a foot-long hot dog is a fairly unusual item; and you know that a self-propelled lawn motor is easier to use and will save the user time that can be spent in other and more enjoyable ways.

Your own knowledge, combined with a check of the Copy Basics in Chapter 12, usually is a sufficient foundation on which to build powerful copy that will move your listeners to action. But it is necessary to make a **conscious** review of your knowledge, point by point, rather than merely assuming that the one detail you need will automatically come to you.

Look at the merchandise, examine the service. Know what you're selling.

It is helpful, actually, to see the merchandise, the store, or the vital aspects of the service for which you write copy. When you go into a department store and feel the materials, look at the styling, evaluate quality on the basis of your own knowledge, experience, and comparison, you can do a far better job of moving your listeners. As a staff copywriter tied down to a desk, you find it impractical many times to get away from your office. As a staff salesman or manager, of course, you are on the scene. When and if it is practical, you will find that you produce more effective copy after you see for yourself.

Stations that do the best jobs for department stores in all size markets have a copywriter assigned to work with store buyers and executives as needed. In a market of 20,000 or less, about three-quarters of one day a week can be sufficient. About half the time is spent in the store inspecting merchandise and discussing plans and ideas with store personnel; the other half is spent writing the week's copy. The copywriter, in this situation, is doubling as account executive and bears considerable responsibility for the course of relations between the station and the store. In a city of 75,000 and larger, it usually is desirable for one person to devote almost full time to a major department store account.

Whatever the practicality, it is highly desirable that you have a first-hand knowledge of the product you're selling, just as it is necessary for a salesman to have a thorough knowledge of what he's selling when he's face to face with his prospect.

One of the prime motivating factors in restaurant copy is atmosphere. How can you know what that atmosphere is until you actually walk in as a customer, sit at a table, scan the menu, order, and then experience the service and food? A knowledgeable restaurant manager (and they're even rarer than knowledgable copywriters) would invite you to sample his product before you write copy for it. Not only invite, but insist.

An alert station manager might send a copywriter at station expense to sample a restaurant for which he wants speculative copy. That's the way to get a great spec tape that motivates a prospect to close and close now.

HOW TO AIM YOUR POWER COPY LIKE A RIFLE AT YOUR CLIENT'S PROSPECTS.

After analyzing store or product appeal, your next step is to determine who, among your listeners, these appeals would affect the most. Who, among your listeners, would be most receptive to the appeals you have decided are the strongest.

If your client is a department store advertising "Ladies spring dresses, $7.95 value for only $5.29," the first question you must answer is "who buys $7.95 dresses?" This narrows your field considerably since it is immediately obvious that you can eliminate wives of doctors, lawyers, dentists, college professors, and business executives whose incomes normally are well above the $12,000 line.

Depending on your own knowledge and the characteristics of your market, chances are you can eliminate the majority of career girls who work in the offices of substantial businesses.

That leaves the big middle majority of housewives whose family incomes are mostly under $10,000. After arriving at that fairly simple conclusion, you then direct your copy to the average housewife who is concerned with keeping her wardrobe in style, but who must pinch pennies to do it.

Whether the product is furniture, automobiles, houses in a new development, or any other item, you must first determine what type of people can be expected to buy it. Your client is the best source of that information.

After analyzing the product appeals, determine how they can be presented to the type of person who listens to your station or to the type of person for whom they are intended. This is a relatively simple step. In the case of the $7.95 dresses on sale at $5.29, you have determined that your prospects are middle income housewives with emphasis on the lower end of that scale.

What kind of appeal is effective to a lower middle housewife? Consider the possibilities:

A. Does she want high fashion appropriate for jet-set society?

No!

B. Does she want the mod styles of Carnaby Street?

No!

C. Does she want dreary, tasteless dresses with no relation to current style?

No!

D. Well, then, what does she want?

Wouldn't she like to know where she can select from a wide variety of tasteful, attractive dresses designed for the life she leads, but with some obvious clue that ties them to this years' styles—at a saving of $2.66?

Like her husband who looks longingly at a $6,000 Thunderbird or Jaguar, she may lavish many wistful hours on boutique copies of Dior's dreams. But like her husband who knows that his daily trip to the factory parking lot justifies no more than a two-year-old Ford, she has no place to go where the Paris look would be appropriate. Both dream of way out glory but settle for dreary practicality with enough cash left over to buy chuck roast, hamburger, and an occasional fifth of bourbon.

What about your banker who wants to increase his share of the automobile loan market? Who are his prospects? First, you can eliminate everybody who neither owns nor wants an automobile. But that's not much help: 87 percent of the families in the United States own cars. Virtually all of them will continue trading cars and making payments to banks and finance companies the rest of their lives. Almost every man above the age of 18 (many younger) is a prospect or desperately wants to be. Many single girls who work are prospects. Young couples, both of whom have jobs and need separate transportation, may be potential purchasers. Many families are ready for a second or third car.

Auto loans have almost as wide a market as bread, toothpaste and soap. Realistically, the banker's prospects are only those who can qualify for bank credit. Banks, for the most part, are much easier to deal with than in the more conservative days and actively seek the business of almost anyone who has a steady job.

What about supermarkets? Who are prospects for them? First, eliminate segments of your audience who obviously cannot use the products and conveniences of a supermarket: Most single men and single girls who live away from home; they're more likely to be restaurant prospects. Eliminate children and teenagers. But that's as far as you can go. Every family living in a house or apartment with a kitchen is a supermarket prospect.

Further eliminations are made only with respect to territory. Some families in your listening area may live too far from your supermarket client to be prime prospects. But good broadcast advertising copy has pulled grocery shoppers from a 30-mile radius in many markets. Similar reasoning and the elimination of certain types of listeners can bring you right on target for almost any advertiser.

Many times it is necessary to write two kinds of copy for the same client.

When a department store is promoting a store-wide sale, there will be items of interest to men, others exclusively to women, and still others of almost exclusive interest to older teenagers or the student group. Still, the lady of the house is likely to buy for any or all other members of her family.

In auto advertising, different language or a shift in attitude may be desirable in offering identical merchandise to different groups: high school and college students, and older, more conservative adults. The appeals of size and luxury are the same to all groups, but a lighter, breezier, attitude is likely to be more effective with the younger men.

THE BUSINESS ANALYSIS FORM

The business analysis form in Chapter 13, when completed with the help and advice of your client, gives you invaluable information on which to create a copy platform. In larger markets your clients usually have well-established images (at least in their own estimation) and you have that as a basis for your copy philosophy.

In smaller markets an image is what your client sees in the mirror as he shaves. He's just running a store and hopes you're going to send him some customers. The way you do it is not vitally important to him. He's not going to complain about how you do it if you get results; by the same token he's not likely to give you credit when you do. In that kind of situation, as well as in larger markets where good business practices are less rare, the form provides solid information to guide your analysis of prospects and appeals.

The form has been an invaluable tool for salesmen. It is used as a wedge to build confidence and to get the prospect to give useful information about his business. Then the information is used in creating copy for speculative tapes and as a basis for recommending a definite plan or campaign.

Chet Ternes, local sales manager at WSUB, Groton, Conn., reports highly gratifying results from the form. It helps create confidence on the part of the prospect and, when the information is fed back to him as part of the station's recommendation, he is impressed with what he believes must be the vast amount of independent research you have done. The average advertiser appears to be unaware of the value of the information he is giving in response to questions on the form.

"I feel that the great usefulness of this form," Chet said, "stems from the fact that most businessmen don't like advertising but realize that it is necessary and they appreciate having someone take most of the worry of it off their hands."

"Which would you rather buy from," Chet concluded, "a radio gypsy who always has a fast deal, or someone who'll handle it all for you?"

Make notes on the form as to basic appeals or the probability and ways that appeals will vary. This will save much time in analyzing all the information in each form every time you write copy for the client.

HOW TO SELECT ONE OF THE MANY TYPES OF COPY FOR MAXIMUM POWER.

There are several possible types of copy which might produce results for your client. Ability to select the one that can produce the best results is part of the skill of a professional copywriter.

REVIEW your knowledge of the business.
Is it:

A. Prestige business such as a financial institution, utility, school, department store, or specialty shop?

B. Staple, everyday type business such as a supermarket, service station, promotion department store or specialty shop, hardware store, or restaurant?

C. Promotion type business depending on daily or weekly promotion effort?

REVIEW possible types of copy that you might use. Some types discussed here are most generally useful with department store and specialty shop advertising policies, but all are useful in almost all types of businesses.

There are two broad classes of copy:

A. Institutional

B. Promotional

Institutional copy can be further classified as:

A. Service

B. Prestige

Promotional copy can be further classified as:

A. Regular price line

B. Bargain

Institutional copy is used to build the image of the product, business, store, or department.

A. **Service copy** publicizes policies, customer services, conveniences, and features of superiority.

B. **Prestige copy** emphasizes the desirability of a product, service, or merchandise, such as the fashion alertness of a store or the wide assortment available. Prestige copy invites shopping when the listener is ready.

Promotional copy is used to promote day-to-day business. It invites the listener to buy now when the advertiser wants him to buy.

A. **Regular price line copy** promotes regular merchandise at established prices. Price, while important, is subordinate to appeals of quality, usefulness, and other characteristics.

B. **Bargain copy** is used where price is the dominant appeal. In general retailing it is divided into: **special promotion** and **clearance**.

Special promotion copy promotes merchandise specially purchased with price concessions, distress merchandise, seconds, irregulars, etc., or merchandise reduced from stock.

Clearance copy promotes left-overs from regular stock or from special promotions.

Other classifications of copy are based on the type of merchandise and your technique of motivation.

A. **Fashion copy** offers information about merchandise, explaining that it is fashionable and why. Mostly used in department store and specialty shop advertising for women's fashions, it is also consistently used in automobile copy. It also is useful in promoting furniture, home decor, lawn mowers, boats, and fishing tackle.

B. **Utility copy** normally is concerned with merchandise of a staple character, which is bought because of its inherent usefulness rather than because it is a current style or fad. Washing machines, dryers, air conditioners, refrigerators, vacuum cleaners, and household linen fall in this category. Both price and quality are emphasized.

Remember, however, in writing any type of copy for any product or business, there may be, and probably is, some hidden motivation involved.

One kitchen range manufacturer, as a result of a survey of housewives, learned that they wanted larger ranges in order to have plenty of work space on top. The manufacturer promptly designed and marketed a range with the same amount of work space as the largest models but which occupied a much smaller floor space.

Sales were disappointing.

Motivational research then disclosed that what housewives actually want in a range is not the work space, but the appearance of luxury that a large range gives the kitchen. The manufacturer brought out a large range, lavished with luxury features, and sales zoomed.

Copy for kitchen ranges, must of course, stress utility, convenience, and quality construction. But it also should include references to a big, luxurious appearance. The same type of motivations probably carry over into other large appliances, including washers and dryers.

*

MOST COPY CAN BE FURTHER CLASSIFIED

Most copy you write falls into one of the three following classifications or a combination of two or more of them:

1. Reason-why copy

2. Human-interest copy

3. Rationalization copy

Good motivational, hard-selling promotional copy usually is a combination of reason-why and rationalization. Human interest copy normally takes too long for a straight pitch—that is, one announcer making a pitch directly to YOU the listener. But in dramatized production copy, human interest is, of course, the most valuable and is inherent in that form.

Reason-why Copy can be further classified as:

1. Testimonial copy

2. Performance copy

3. Test copy

4. Construction copy

Testimonial copy features a purchaser or user of the merchandise who tells of its desirability in his own voice, but sometimes in your words. A good local testimonial is most effective. It is especially useful and obtainable in farm-use products (feed, fertilizer, implements, etc.). Samples appear in Chapter 13. Sometimes it is desirable for the copywriter, account executive, manager, or program director to spend half a day or more with a client's representative, visiting a series of users and recording their comments for later editing and splicing into well-organized commercials.

Performance copy expounds on the ability of a product to stand up under use or to produce superior performance. This type of copy convinces because it is **specific.** Shell's TV commercials demonstrate this perfectly. The viewer is told: "you get more mileage with Shell **because** Shell has Platformate." Then the demonstration shows exactly how much more mileage identical cars on the same course get using Shell with Platformate. That is specific. That is proof. It cannot be denied without charging the company with outright lying and the company officers with conspiracy. It is convincing because it is specific.

Such test results are rarely available for use in local retail copy, but an alert copywriter finds some effective way to dramatize an occasional product or store. It has been found, for instance, that the average white-collar worker walks an average of 17,000 steps a day. The cuffs of his trousers often wear out first because of the 17,000 times a day they rub lightly together. A material that will withstand that constant light abrasion is good fodder for dramatization in test copy. Your finished commercial might well begin like this:

ANNCR: If you wear a coat and tie to work, this sound is important to you. Listen!

SOUND: (swish swish swish)

ANNCR: That's the sound of your trouser cuffs wearing out. Quite often cuffs are the first places to show wear in a perfectly good suit (and on into details of hard-finished material and why it lasts longer).

Test copy is somewhat similar. It also convinces by the specific nature of the information. Authentic test results usually come only from recognized testing laboratories or the Good Housekeeping Institute. Shell copy is a combination of test as well as performance copy.

Construction copy describes the way the product is made. It offers no proof based on tests or experience and, consequently, is not as effective as testimonial, performance, and test copy. But in the absence of proof, which is the usual situation at station level, it is helpful to point out specific construction features, explaining how each adds value, strength, expands usefulness, etc.

Reason-why copy is the most widely useful in retail advertising because it is direct, logical, interests only potential customers, gets to the point fast, and gives solid reasons for buying. Reason-why copy can be written in either straight pitch or production form.

A disadvantage of writing straight pitch reason-why copy is that it tends to become monotonous as a style, when considered and heard as part of the day's programming with other straight pitch spots. It is the least glamorous of all the types of copy. However, when used in conjunction with imaginative production techniques and writing, it can be brilliant.

Human interest copy appeals to emotions and sense rather than to intellect and judgment. Sympathy, affection, fear, humor, curiosity, and other emotional appeals are used as well as appeals to the sense of sight, touch, taste, smell, and hearing. It relates merchandise to people. Normally, it takes a more leisurely pace and, before the advent of practical tape-handling equipment, it was more suited to print media. Now, however, human interest is the basis of most of the very best broadcast copy written.

Human interest copy is likely to create more intense interest than other types because people are interested in people. As Victor Hugo once noted, "Emotion is always new." Human interest copy is likely to be more exciting and unusual than reason-why copy and it is a refreshing change to your listeners. Dialog copy featuring two or more people in conversation about a product or promotion is a simple form of human interest copy.

Human interest copy may be further classified into four types:

1. Humorous copy
2. Fear copy
3. Story copy
4. Predicament copy

Humor should be confined to those products and businesses where the client has given prior approval to a humorous approach. Many good jobs have been lost because of a client's disapparoval of impromptu humor. A business owner sees nothing funny about his business. It is a serious matter on which his future and the future of his family depends. The vast majority of businessmen are extremely sensitive about humor in connection with their businesses. An employed manager or executive is even more sensitive in that respect because of his fear of a superior's reaction against him.

Humor is the most difficult of all copy to do well and should be attempted only by writers who have a natural bent for it. After humor copy has been taped, unless it has been done by a writer (as well as talent) who has had much successful experience with humor, it should be given an honest test against the sensibilities of more than one layman. Another station employee does not constitute a test. His reaction is inclined to be based on personal bias; for the sake of future relationships within the staff, he is inclined to laugh it up and pronounce judgment that both copy and production are great. The opinion of a store clerk or a service station manager who gives you a blank look and says, honestly, "I don't get it!" is worth more than all the yaks you can milk from the station staff.

Charles Brewer, general manager, WHIN, Gallatin, Tennessee, and an excellent writer of humor copy, recommends beginning with a punch line, then writing to it. You'll see some of his copy in this book.

Fear copy generally has little, if any, usefulness in retail advertising. Some reliance is occasionally placed on it in national advertising for insurance and tires. On the local level a more positive approach is likely to produce best results. Motivational research has disclosed that other appeals strike a more responsive chord among the strings of human emotion. Some of these appear in Chapter 12.

One prime principle to remember in writing copy for anything, is this:

EXHAUSTIVE TESTS HAVE INDICATED CONCLUSIVELY

THAT A CURE OUTSELLS A PREVENTIVE BY FAR.

Story copy in dialog form is a most useful and effective technique. The characters you create for your dialog tell the client's story of benefits in natural fashion and can inject any emotion you wish into the taped commercial. The many possibilities inherent in dialog copy are taken up in detail later.

Predicament copy crosses the lines of both human interest and story copy. The predicament may be humorous, use the psychology of fear, or may simply be (as most such commercials are) a fictitious dialog or story. Its purpose is to point out benefits in a dramatic manner.

Rationalization copy, when used with a practical knowledge of hidden motivations can be expected to produce the best results. It combines reason-why with human interest. It is by far the most effective technique in selling almost everything.

It works to whet the appetite of a $100-a-week shipping clerk for a 521½ hp automobile with power ash trays and Hide-a-bed; then tells him the extra power gives him "an extra margin of safety" (that he wouldn't need if he didn't have surplus power in the first place) and that the Hide-a-bed is indispensible for "the few minutes daily relaxation that doctors recommend" for the hard-charging young businessman.

Similar techniques sell refrigerators, washing and drying machines, lawn mowers, clothing, real estate, boats, airplanes, and virtually all consumer items.

Now that all the fuzzy-minded idealists have been flushed out of the Utopian bushes by the preceding paragraphs, let us get on with the business of increasing the distribution of the GNP. Frank Bettger, one of the nation's twelve Master Salesmen, says that he decided early in his career that he would spend the rest of his life finding out what his prospects want and then helping them to get it. The same principle is the foundation of a master copywriter.

It has been said that the perfect, invincible sales approach is first to

EMOTIONALIZE,

then

RATIONALIZE!

Here are several practical examples of the technique:

New instant tea tastes great (emotional appeal to one of the five senses) **because** it's flavored with lemon (the rationalization).

Ford's new Maverick is ideal for a young couple's first car because it is bigger and more luxurious than the Volkswagen, yet the price is almost as low.

Now is the time to buy a new self-propelled lawn mower because this 1971 model, direct-drive, with 3½ hp Briggs & Stratton motor and handlebar controls is on sale today and tomorrow at a $10 saving.

You always save money at Belk's because buyers buy for 300 stores, getting lower prices, which they pass right on to you.

INSTITUTIONAL COPY

To be effective, institutional copy usually must come from an idea such as the business' slogan or the concept of an image it wants to build. Cain-Sloan, in Nashville, constantly hammers on the idea that it is the "greatest store in the Central South, where selections are complete." This copy is embodied in a jingle that follows much of the store's radio copy.

One of New York's great department stores, Macy's, has its slogan engraved in a concrete plaque high above its main entrance. "It's smart to be thrifty" is used in all the store's advertising.

Copy must grow from the idea. It must be friendly and can be humorous or musical. Its only purpose is to win friends.

BARGAIN COPY

Bargain copy is no easier or faster to write than any other kind, and indeed, may be more difficult in many cases. Good bargain copy requires a serious study of the possible motivating factors involved, since price alone is not a motivation.

Remember that your housewife prospect is not going to rush down to the promotion store to buy "four pairs of ladies panties for a dollar," because she has ants in her pants to spend a dollar. If her motivation were simply to spend a dollar she could get it out of her system probably a lot closer to home. Her motivation to buy is based on what the merchandise will do for her. Some of the things it might do for her are:

1. Feel silky and luxuriously feminine
2. Last through two years of machine washing
3. Provide colors she needs for ensembles
4. Bring her supply up to match that of her nosey sister-in-law.

Barnum was right: There is a sucker born every minute. But they're more sophisticated than in the days of that great showman. Today's typical housewife, while rather unknowing in regard to wide problems of politics and philosophy, is a tower of judgment compared to the hayseeds of Barnum's time. The typical middle majority housewife, according to much research regarding her mentality, activities, and motivations, tends to be quite dull and dreary, devoting virtually all her thought and energy to her home and family.

She is unlikely to have any logical, thought-out opinion or guiding philosophy on such subjects as war, the draft, welfare, socialism, or legalizing abortion, pot, and prostitution. But she is savvy enough to know there's no such thing as a free lunch. When you tell her Murphy's Department Store is holding the granddaddy of all gigantic sales this week and that she should rush right down and buy a $99 coat with mink trim and sterling silver buttons for $39.95, she immediately wants to know how come. "How come they want to sell a $99 coat for $39.95," is her first reaction. "There must be something wrong with it," is her second.

There's something wrong with a copywriter who fails adequately to explain why that $99 coat can now be bought for $39.95. Some possible reasons are:

1. It must be cleared out to make room for new spring fashions.

2. It was part of an over-run the store bought from the factory at distress prices.

3. The store has a sharp buyer who knows where and how to get fabulous bargains like this for you.

4. It is part of a lot bought from a bankrupt store in Pasadena.

5. The store made a mistake and bought too many. Now they've got to go and prices have been slashed to a new low.

Doesn't that make Mrs. D. D. Housewife feel better about the whole thing? She knows now that there's nothing wrong with it; she knows it's new and in first class condition; and she knows that it is, indeed, a real bargain and that the buyer's mistake (or astuteness) is a break for her. She may just run down and see if they have a red one in her size.

Good Practices in Writing Bargain Copy

Good advertising practice requires that copy describe the merchandise accurately and specifically. When price comparisons are used they should be truthful and subject to proof. Otherwise, the store is likely to incur lasting customer dissatisfaction.

Accuracy and truthfulness, especially in small-market promotion stores, usually are beyond the control of the station copywriter. It must be recognized that often the copywriter, who may well be the manager or a salesman, is simply handed a list of "specials" written on the back of a bank's counter check with oral instructions to "run me 10 spots on these tomorrow."

It also must be recognized that the opportunity to follow good advertising practices is often circumvented by store managers who equate a one-minute spot with the space of half a newspaper page and insist upon a price list with opening and closing.

Immediate sales is the goal of bargain copy and your copy must contain what a salesman calls a "hooker" to motivate buying now. The hooker is simply a reason. Usually, in bargain copy a hooker is the price. Or the fact that the sale ends tomorrow. In selling transistor radios or TV sets a hooker could be a promise to deliver in time for the world series or a moon shot. It doesn't have to be a world-shaker. Remember, to the prospective buyer who is receptive, any excuse is better than none.

In bargain copy you must sell the idea that now is the time to buy, just as you sell the merchandise. You must promise the prospect some benefit that will come only from buying now. Emotionalize the benefits of the merchandise and then rationalize the necessity of buying now.

You might write "Sears announces a sale for exactly 103 women," explaining that prices on 103 dresses have been marked down, etc. You can describe the time of the sale "two days only" or "weekend sale" or "this week." You can spur early action by stressing "shop Sears today for the best selection." Near the end of the sale you can spur action by urging: "Go now! The sale ends at 5 PM tomorrow," or you can give your copy immediacy with: "Size and color selections are getting smaller every hour. Go now and choose the dresses you want at this fantastic price."

REGULAR PRICE LINE

Regular price line copy is based on a combined appeal, stemming from both quality (or characteristics) and price. As

Maurice Rayfield, astute merchandiser at Seligman's Department Store, Bastrop, La., explains, "We're selling fashion at a price."

The purpose is to induce immediate sales of regular stock merchandise at established prices. This copy emphasizes style, fashion, construction, workmanship, brand name, and points of superiority. It creates a favorable impression so that the customer will remember when she is ready to buy. There is a combination of both promotional and institutional advertising in this, since the response you're aiming for is both immediate and lasting.

SUMMARY

To find the maximum POWER appeal, ask yourself:

A. What is the greatest benefit of buying?

B. What are the secondary benefits?

C. Check your Copy Basics in Chapter 12.

D. Check national advertising.

E. Review your own knowledge of the product or business.

F. Examine the merchandise personally.

Aim your copy like a rifle at prospects. Ask yourself:

A. Who, among our listeners, would be most receptive to these appeals?

B. How can these appeals best be presented?

Use the business analysis form for a permanent record of the client's appeals.

Review various types of copy and select the one which offers the BEST opportunity for effective presentation of buying motivations.

Classifications are:

A. Fashion copy

B. Utility copy

C. Further classifications:

    1. Reason-why copy
        a. Testimonial
        b. Performance
        c. Test
        d. Construction

    2. Human interest copy

    3. Rationalization copy

A combination of reason-why and rationalization is most widely useful.

D. Institutional copy, usually, must come from an idea such as the store slogan or an image it wants to build. There are two types:

    1. Service

    2. Prestige

E. Promotional copy is based on specific merchandise and invites the listener to buy now, when the store wants her to. Not necessarily bargain copy, but price is important even if subordinate to the characteristics of the merchandise.

F. Bargain copy must explain the reason for a low price, as well as give some motivating reason to buy. Price alone is no motivation. If the motive were only to save money, the customer could stay home and save even more. It should include motivation to buy **now**.

G. Regular price line copy emphasizes the characteristics of the merchandise, but uses a reference to the low price to induce immediate action. It also seeks to establish a favorable and lasting impression.

Chapter 3

How To Put Power Into Your Opening

The most important element of your copy is the opening, or lead—the leading sentence. It must grab the attention of your prospects so they will hear the remainder of your copy. Otherwise, your entire effort is wasted. You must do something in your lead to compel your prospects to listen. There are many variations of this technique but they are all directed to the same purpose.

GET ATTENTION

Batten, Barton, Durstine & Osborn advertising agency produced an award-winning commercial for New England Bell Telephone that didn't have a word in it for the first 30 seconds. It was a highly effective story in sound. Many stations subscribe to transcription services that provide attention-compelling sounds and other aids. These can be very helpful to a copywriter who knows what he wants to accomplish with sound.

The telephone commercial was directed toward building the idea of obtaining convenience from residential phone service. It accomplished its purpose with a series of sounds that told the story of inconvenience and frustration. It began with a loud sawing sound. Then a telephone began ringing faintly in the distance. The sawing sound stopped, followed by running footsteps. A hollowness in the footstep sounds then indicated a flight of stairs. The hollow sound again changed to a more solid floor. Finally, as the intensity of the telephone bell indicated that the runner had reached the room in which it was located, there was the sound of the receiver being lifted and an out-of-breath man's voice saying "hello." The dial tone came through, loud and clear, indicating that the man who had run from his basement, up the stairs, and down the hall to reach the ringing phone, had been too late. A 30-second pitch for adding an extension phone followed.

Several points can be made for this award-winner.

1. The attention-compeller was unusual and identifiable. Not only did it compel attention, it also told a story in and of itself.

2. The attention-compeller involved human-interest. It began with the sound of a person wielding a handsaw, raising the question of what is going on. Curiosity!

3. The human interest increased as the sawing stopped and the running footsteps began. The listener is hooked, wondering if the runner will get to the phone in time or what he will hear after he gets there.

4. The listener is involved in the unspoken story, just as he would be in a published short story, as the running footsteps reach the phone and the receiver is lifted. There is suspense. And it has reached a moment of climax. What will happen to resolve this little drama that features a **conflict** between the man and the phone?

5. The dial tone tells the story: Utter frustration that every listener has experienced. The listener recognizes the plight of the runner and shares some of the frustration. The listener has become emotionally involved in the fictional situation. He is now receptive to comments and suggestions based on that involvement. The writer of this excellent and wordless piece of motivation first **emotionalized**, then **rationalized** by suggesting a **cure** for the problem.

6. After the 30-second story-in-sound, the copy offered a solution by suggesting that the listener install an extension phone in the basement. Forty-four words did it for this one-minute spot.

In presenting that commercial before a group of Georgia radio men, Martin Hollinger, media director for the Atlanta office of BBD&O, remarked that radio should be evaluated on the basis of what it can do for each individual product.

A 30-second story-in-sound is not a technique that can be adapted to every radio advertiser, and, just as obviously, the point was made better by radio than it could have been in any other medium. Sound was all that was needed. Sight would have been a detracting factor.

IMAGINATION

The listener's imagination is one of the greatest ingredients of good radio copy. You can show your listeners the most beautiful, romantic, awe-inspiring or horrifying sights in the world any time you wish.

Here's the way Lou Nelson uses that principle to create a scene on main street in a town of the old west. Notice the scene of unpainted, false-fronted buildings, hitching racks in front of each, and the dusty street. Lou did it without a hammer, nail, or bulldozer. Listen!

SOUND: **STINGER**

LOU: **(TENSE, DRAMATIC MONOTONE) One day a gunfighter, all dressed in black, rode into Dover.**

You can do it, too. All you need is one sheet of paper that costs less than one cent, a typewriter, and your own imagination. You can show your listeners—as easily as the BBD&O copywriter showed the frustration of that situation—the joys of driving into Bob Smith's Westside Texaco, or dining at a fine restaurant, or enjoying a fast drive-in hamburger, or wearing a light, bright spring dress. The limits of what you can do in that respect are defined by only three factors:

1. Good (or at least, acceptable) taste

2. Your client's approval (actual or tacit)

3. Your own knowledge and imagination

You can make a man feel the tremendous sense of power that comes from driving a 521½ hp automobile with four on the floor, Hedder headers, and Phooter footers. You can give your woman listener something of the thrill of trying on a new bathing suit that will make her the Belle of the Beach, or a $3,500 mink that makes her feel loved in the lap of luxury.

If this seems a little far out for a station copywriter's talents, consider what you could do very simply on a sweltering July afternoon by writing (and airing) something like this:

ANNCR: **Good afternoon ladies and gentlemen. This is Joe Bloe speaking to you from high above the fifty-yard line here at Legion Field where in just a few moments Ted Husing and Bill Stern will describe the play-by-play action in the game between the Albuquerque Jackrabbits and the Miami Porpoises. But first a word from the Smothers Brothers who are hanging by** their teeth underneath a giant Cheyene helicopter circling slowly over the field. They'll have to talk fast because when they open their mouths they'll drop. But if all goes well they'll drop into that big portable Esther Williams swimming pool that's being trundled along underneath their helicopter. Oh! We're about to have some action. Tom Smothers is signaling frantically for the tractor driver to bring the swimming pool forward...looks like the helicopter is moving too fast for the tractor. OOOOOOH ...HE'S DROPPING! Tom Smothers is dropping from 500 feet. Is this a show business stunt? Or is he really dropping to his death before 115,000 football fans...

In less than 60 seconds you could become the poor man's Orson Welles. Abraham Lincoln said it: "You can fool all of the people some of the time..."

As a station copywriter you have limitless opportunities to use your "fooling" ability in a constructive manner, convincing many thousands of people that your advertisers' merchandise will make them more powerful, beautiful, efficient, competent, attractive, sexy; improve their posture, appearance, personality, teeth, health, social position, or accomplish almost anything else that may be experienced only in their most private dreams.

Notice that the reference to "your fooling ability" suggests "fooling" your listener into a predetermined mood, a mood to appreciate the merchandise you are selling on your client's behalf. It is not intended to suggest that you fool your listeners by telling untruths or half-truths about the merchandise.

You can do it as simply as you could paint a word picture of the intrepid tractor driver, who turns out to be Dean Martin, wearing red Mandarin pajamas and a white turban, producing a roar of power and a spurt of speed to bring the swimming pool into place as Tom Smothers does a triple somersault, tops it with a backward jacknife and sails into the Olympic-size pool with a swan dive.

In the mad scramble of day-to-day (or minute-to-minute) station operation, it is easy to lose sight of the basic purpose of copywriting, which is simply to "make 'em want it." Remember, the way to send your listeners to your client's store is to paint a word picture of the listener enjoying the benefits (as the listener sees those benefits) of the merchandise. Here's the way Lou Nelson painted a picture of the benefits available at Morristown Ford.

EDDIE: (COLD) Hey, Joe. Do you tink I have charisma?

JOE: Gee, I dunno, Eddie. Have you been to a doctor?

EDDIE: Man, dis is not nuttin' medical. It's kind of a maggotism some people or tings have. In fact, dat new T-bird you bought recently from Morristown Ford. Now, dat turns me on.

JOE: It does?

EDDIE: Sure, but de only ting is, you hadda pay over six grand for dat 69 at Morristown Ford.

JOE: Six grand? Not me man. I wouldn't go for six big ones. Not only dat, I don't have dat kind of dough.

EDDIE: You didn't pay six Gs for dat 69 T-Bird and you got all do accessories,"da"air conditioning, da power all around, da stereo radio, da whitewalls, da whole bit?

JOE: Yeah, I got all dat and more. But I paid less than five for it. In fact, I saved more than $1,200 bucks off the list price, which was $6103.

EDDIE: You mean you paid sump'n like $4,800 for your new 69 T-bird?

JOE: Yeah, sump'n like dat.

EDDIE: Joe, I have come to a conclusion. You have charisma.

JOE: I do?

EDDIE: I don't have charisma.

JOE: You don't?

EDDIE: I know how I can get charisma.

JOE: You do?

EDDIE: You don't unnerstand.

JOE: I don't?

EDDIE: Not havin' dat 69 T-bird from Morristown Ford was keepin' me from realizin' my full potential.

JOE: Hop into my charisma and let me drive you down to Morristown Ford and let's pick out yours.

PRICE ALONE IS INSUFFICIENT MOTIVATION

If your prospect's purpose is simply to save money, he can stay home and save more than if he went downtown to buy the bargain-priced, money-saving merchandise. Certainly the price-only motivation will attract prospects who have already made up their minds that they want similar merchandise. But thousands more who do not actively want it are left totally unmoved by the recitation of the price list. When a promotion type store advertises a list like this:

One group of ladies' dresses, $14.95 value, only $10.29

One group of girls' panty hose, $1.98 value, only $1.19

One group of ladies' bras, $2.98 value, only $2.29

One group of boys' shoes, values from $4.99 to $8.00, only $4.49

Every framed picture in the store reduced 20 percent.

there is nothing to motivate a prospect who has not already made up her mind that she wants one or more of those items. A separate one-minute spot devoted to each of the groups would move more prospects to want, and subsequently buy. J. C. Penney Co. maintains that policy by providing recorded spots for local use. They are among the most effective broadcast advertisers on the air in small and medium markets.

Picture Mrs. Middle Majority Housewife, wearing her nightgown and second best dressing robe, standing at the over-sized kitchen range (the one she bought because its size adds to the luxurious appearance of her kitchen) turning the breakfast eggs in her Teflon skillet with her special plastic spatula.

"Hush, Junior. I want to hear about Belk's sale. They never have anything on sale I want, but I don't want to miss anything."

So she listens to the transistor radio setting on the Formica-topped dinette table and hears a price list.

"Same old stuff," she says, halfway to herself. "I didn't want to go downtown today, anyway."

And so she stays home and saves her money instead of going to Belk's and spending $10.29 to save $4.66. She heard nothing to motivate her to want any of the merchandise listed.

In contrast to the price list copy, imagine taking the group of $14.95 value dresses and developing 60 seconds of selling copy. Again Mrs. M. M. Housewife is poised over the luxurious-appearing kitchen range with plastic spatula to turn the breakfast eggs. Coming from the transistor is an idea that grabs her attention and also arouses considerable interest. Some feminine voices are admiring something that must also be feminine. She learns immediately that the object of admiration is a dress. Mrs. Housewife is definitely interested in dresses. She listens intently.

FEMININE VOICES:	Oh, how adorable.
	It's beautiful.
	And just look at that delicate work on the yoke.
SOUND:	Mrs. Housewife gives Junior an urgent "Shhhhhh," and pauses between range and table, spatula in mid air.
FEMININE VOICE:	I'm so glad you like it. When I saw it at Belk's I just couldn't resist. I took it off the rack and held it up at the mirror and it looked just like me.
OTHER FEMININE VOICE:	Oh, it is you, Beth. It is you. So perfect.
BETH:	Then I tried it on. It felt just like a breath of spring.

Here, Mrs. Housewife begins to get the idea that there is something desirable about those dresses on sale today and tomorrow at Belk's. Depending on what else she hears, she might just run downtown today, after all, and see if she can find one that is her before they're all gone. She identifies her own desires, longings, and needs (psychological and social as well as physical) with those of the voices. When the suggestion is properly made in any one of many ways, it is implanted in her mind and begins to grow.

The suggestion, subsequently, is watered and fed by the additional impressions planted in other commercials. While she may be skeptical after the first impression, by the time she has heard another one as she's putting the breakfast dishes in the sink to be washed at some more convenient time, and a third as she drives Junior to school, and a fourth as she returns and pulls into her own driveway, she may have the feeling that her plans for the day revolve around a trip to Belk's to find one of those $14.95 dresses for $10.29 that is her.

The perhaps small desire created by the first impression is reinforced by subsequent impressions. Mere repetition of the price list does nothing to reinforce her desire because she doesn't have the desire in the first place. There's nothing to reinforce.

Consequently, a lead that merely urges her to save, save, save at Belk's gigantic sale, etc., is short of the mark. She is neither a PhD nor a Phi Beta Kappa, but she's smart enough to know that the best place to save her money is a bank. You can't entice her to Belk's for the purpose of saving her money. You can, however, easily entice her to Belk's with a promise that she'll find something that contributes to her ultimate happiness by making her feel as fresh as a breath of spring. The fact that she can save $4.66 by deciding now is a strong factor in her decision. These two factors, then, can be used as the foundation for an urge to save, save save. But you must make it clear in the lead and elsewhere in the copy that you are suggesting a move toward her happiness, not confusing a department store with a bank.

The above explanation is both exaggerated and over-simplified, but the point is valid. Lure her to Belk's with a promise of the benefit that she is likely to value the most. In the case of a sale or reduced prices, it is well to mention it in the lead along with the primary benefit. If a choice must be made between the benefit and the reduced price in the lead, always feature the benefit first.

NARROW YOUR FIELD

If you do nothing else with your lead, make certain that it grabs the attention of your prospects; prospects, not necessarily all listeners. Grab the attention of only the listeners who are prospects. This is simply differentiation in your own selfish interest. For the one minute that this commercial is on the air you have no concern whatsoever with people who are not prospects. If the product is brassieres, you couldn't care less whether or not you get the attention of men listeners. But you do want all women listeners to hear what you have to say. If the product is maternity brassieres, then you are concerned only with women in the age bracket of perhaps 18 to 36 and who, let us hope, are married. This narrows the field somewhat, as does each additional qualification you add to the description of your prospects. The process of elimination will eventually bring you down to the exact focal point—which is your group of prospects. Forget everyone else.

About 1954, a Houston station produced copy for a simple, live commercial for Pearl Beer that made the differentiation as perfectly as it can be done. The lead was short and simple:

ANNCR: (COLD) If you like a good beer..."

It separated immediately the prospects from the non-prospects. Listeners who do not drink beer have no interest in what comes next and it makes no difference whatever because they're not going to buy Pearl or any other beer, no matter what you say about it. Conversely, everyone who drinks beer is attracted to the idea that the announcer is going to say something of direct interest.

There is nothing wrong with having nonprospects hear what you have to say. But you can make the appeal of your lead stronger when you point it directly at prospects, automatically eliminating nonprospects. Put another way, your opening will be strong, will grab the attention of more real prospects, when you point it directly at them with all the psychological power you can bring to bear, ignoring all other listeners for the moment.

Remember, it is easier to sell a pound of cure than an ounce of prevention. People, generally, are inclined to buy more readily when the product is presented as a **solution** to a problem, rather than as a **prevention** of a problem. Notice that there is virtually no retail market for fire extinguishers. Fire extinguishers—a preventive—are mostly bought by institutions which are required by law to have them. Notice, also, that it is virtually impossible to find anyone advertising a preventive for athletes foot, but many are selling cures.

Claude Hopkins, legendary ad man who brought Pepsodent from obscurity to top seller, learned from medical reports that one major cause of tooth decay is the film of bacteria that forms on the teeth. He could just as easily—and more logically—have based his copy platform on the fact that Pepsodent prevents film. Being the advertising genius that he was, he knew that a cure—removal of the film—would far outsell the preventive. That great ad man's marvelous know-how and his understanding of human motivations have been diluted many times by several generations of ad men who followed him on the Pepsodent account. The toothpaste business is a horse race with first one brand leading, then another. But as late as 1957, Pepsodent was still hammering on that film problem with a jingle "You'll wonder where the yellow went, when you brush your teeth with Pepsodent." Variations of the appeal are on the air every week.

It is rarely possible to use **all** effective factors in any one lead, but a good lead should embody **all** these three factors:

1. Appeal to the self-interest of prospects

2. With the right word, phrase, or other sound stimulus

3. Arouse curiosity

Additional factors in a good lead can be:

4. Give news to the point

5. Make it believable

6. Offer quick results

7. Be specific

8. Ease of understanding

9. Contrast

10. Promise benefits

11. Mention product or business favorably

Appeal to the self-interest of your prospects. This is demonstrated perfectly in the Pearl Beer lead, "If you like a good beer..." Pepsi Cola's "Music To Watch Girls By" was another award winner for BBD&O. Beginning with the bright and distinctive music, it faded for the announcer to say in the manner of an emcee introducing a show, "Here's Music To Watch Girls By." It was directed to the youth market and was excellently contrived to grab the attention of all listeners—men and boys who love to watch, and young women and girls who expect to be watched. It did not automatically exclude all the older generation, either, some of whom "think young" as Pepsi was suggesting several seasons earlier.

A department store can appeal to self-interest with something like this:

A. You'll want to look your loveliest when vacation time comes...

B. Start now to build a striking vacation wardrobe.

C. If you're going off to college next fall, you'll want to be sure your wardrobe is right.

D. If you're the thrifty type who insists on every dress being fashion-right for the occasion, but still must economize on your clothes, you'll love the special selection of bright, figure-flattering spring dresses at Belk's this weekend.

E. Belk's announces a two-day sale of dresses for 63 fashion-conscious women.

F. The bright new styles at Belk's this weekend will make you as fresh and desirable as a breath of spring, and you'll save $4.66 on every one.

The right word, phrase, or other sound stimulus, in most cases, is pretty much a matter of individual judgment. If your copy is to be read live on a run-of-station schedule, it must have no strong characteristics that would make it unsuitable for anyone on the board. If, however, it is to be recorded and you have a practical choice of talent, it makes sense to have strictly fashion copy with feminine words done in a woman's voice. With two voices make sure the important points are expressed in feminine words and delivered by a woman's voice.

Bargain copy, where the emphasis is on price, is more appropriate to the harder-selling approach of a male announcer. But here, a confidential Godfrey-type delivery is likely to be more effective than a shouter who simply belts it out in the same tone he would use in selling used car bargains and body shop service. Check for Copy Basics in Chapter 12 for ideas on basic appeals and some suggestions on how to present them.

In Example D above, low price is emphasized initially, but there is appeal to self-interest by using the "right word or phrase." The phrase "you'll love" gets your listener right into the picture by implying that here's something that's great for her. The phrase "bright, figure-flattering dresses" is far better than the uninspiring "special selection of spring dresses," because it tells your prospect what that something great is: it will flatter her figure.

Psychologically, it's the same as telling a woman she's beautiful. Even though she knows that only a damphool could believe it, she's willing to be a tiny bit of a fool because she wants to believe it. And though her plight in the sea of beauty may be as desperate as that of a channel swimmer wearing concrete boots, she still reaches for the straw of believability.

Arouse curiosity. All of the above examples, A through F, tend to arouse curiosity. Some have a stronger effect in that direction than others, but all share the same common denominators of self-interest, right word, phrase or sound. Examples A and B evoke the response "how"? Example C isolates the college students. It could be made stronger, if desirable to do so, by differentiating between boys and girls. As it stands it could be used for either or both. It evokes the response "yes, tell me how." The approach of "I'm going to tell you how," is particularly effective among the college and high school age groups because uncertainty of and concern with dress and etiquette is at its peak.

Example E fairly reeks with curiosity. "Why 63" is the first response. "Could that include me?" is the second. This is a very strong attention compeller. Example F is the weakest in curiosity appeal, but any reference to something that will make a woman feel as "fresh and desirable as a breath of spring" will provoke curiosity and attention.

Give news to the point. Example E gives news: "Belk's announces." The announcer of a (specific) 2-day sale of (more specifics) dresses for 63 fashion-conscious women (most specific) is news of direct interest to fashion-conscious women. It drives straight to the hearts of your prospects because the mention of the store name eliminates the type who wouldn't be caught buying a belt buckle there. At the same time it does attract fashion-conscious women who habitually buy dresses in the $10 to $15 range and know that Belk's is a good source for them.

Make it believable. Examples E and F both employ this factor, in addition to the three necessary common denominators. The mention of a sale for 63 women is specific enough to command belief. The flat statement that "you'll save $4.66 on every one" is also specific enough to be believed without question.

The best key you have to believability is **specifics.** The sale for 63 fashion-conscious women is far more believable than if you use a round figure such as 60, or "more than 60." Test after test, year after year, has confirmed that fact so completely that it is simply taken for granted by advertising pros. Always use a specific figure or fact to increase believability when you can.

A reverse factor that must be considered is that people tend to disbelieve anything that is contrary to their experience. It is possible that the absolute truth will sound like a lie when it offers, without adequate explanation, an unusually good bargain. The term "clearance sale" is sufficient to explain why dresses, furniture, and toys are offered at half price. The same term would not adequately explain how Cadillacs or mink coats or villas in Spain come to be offered at half price. It is contrary to experience.

Offer quick results or fast benefits. The prospect of "fast, fast, fast relief" is fine for a headache remedy. Other quick benefits sometimes are involved in other merchandise. A lead like this might be effective with some prospects:

Honest John will put you in a brand new Buick convertible with radio, power ashtrays, two dummy spotlights, free foxtail, and white sidewalls before the sun sets today.

The "quick results" motivation is indirectly involved in the promotion of a limited-time sale. When the listener hears that the sale ends tomorrow, she understands that quick results is the name of the game if she is going to get any benefit from the event.

Many times the quick results or quick action appeal can give you a little extra power when you use a different basic appeal. Other times, it can be the major thrust of your motivational effort.

Make it easy to understand. All the examples given are easy to understand. They're written directly to the point in simple, everyday language and make no effort to inject an element of mystery, to keep the listener guessing about some far-out concept; they say nothing calculated to confuse or distract her from the main idea. The main idea is, of course, that "Belk's has something that will make you look and feel better, invite compliments, and save you money." The main idea of the Marlboro cigarette commercial was "Filter, Flavor, Pack or Box." What could be easier to understand?

Contrast. Examples D and F offer a bit of contrast that points up value. Contrast is not basic to either, but it adds additional power. There is a bit of contrast between "thrifty type" and "fashion right" because the two characteristics are thought of as being mutually exclusive. There is contrast between "fresh and desirable as a breath of spring" and "save $4.66 on every one." Not as much as in the previous example, but it's there because such factors are normally mutually exclusive.

More effective use of contrast comes from the choice of two words that mean the opposite. Compare the strong contrast in the following examples with the weak contrast in the preceding examples.

Keep your home **cool** and comfortable, even on the **hottest** night.

No matter how **hot** it gets, you can look **cool** and comfortable in...

Bring **exciting** color to a **drab** living room.

Promise benefits. The promise of benefits is inherent in most good leads. Each example of contrast also promises a benefit. This is almost synonymous with the appeal to the self-interest of prospects. But you must be specific in promising benefits. Don't do as a young copywriter in a small-town Georgia station did: "Remember, you get all the benefits of this great new lawn mower."

Mention the product (or business) favorably. Probably the weakest of leads when used alone, this factor does have its place when used in combination with an appeal to self-interest. A good example of the effective use of this type of lead is:

No matter how hot it gets, you can look cool and comfortable in your smartly tailored Palm Beach suit.

In these days of galloping language pollution, it is somewhat of a temptation for younger writers to make the Palm Beach lead read:

"You can keep your cool..."

Except in very unusual cases, it is better to use standard words and terms that can be precisely defined and understood. This subject is discussed at length later.

Writers of mail order advertising must produce copy that sells, and sells now, or they starve. Copy that "keeps the name before the public" is a total waste; their copy must sell now! Experienced mail order copy writers have learned that their business usually is better when their ad or letter begins with what they call "do something" verbs.

A list of headlines (which are comparable to your attention-compelling lead), culled from **Esquire, True, Southern Living** and **Popular Mechanics** magazines, shows the utility of verbs used as stoppers.

STUDY law at home	**FREE** pets of fleas
START your own business	**BUILD** your own summer cottage
Make wine at home	**EARN** while you learn
SEND for the giant catalog	**BUY** it wholesale
DRAW in one day	**BE** a locksmith

Word pictures—created with verbs: **action** words that your prospect can visualize. A man tired of working for someone else can see himself **starting** and enjoying his own business. A man with a green thumb can **see** himself growing miniature trees. Attractive pictures to their prospects, every one!

The style of writing is not always suitable for radio copy, but the basic ideas of hard-selling mail order copy are good for any medium. Mail order copy sells because it must. If your income depended precisely upon the number of customers you send into advertisers' stores, would your copy be stronger than it is?

Chapter 4

The Four-Step Power Plan

The four-step plan in writing copy is based on the four-point AIDA formula. Good copy is developed in this order:

Attention

Interest

Desire

Action

The first step in creating copy is to analyze what you have to sell and determine the appeals, the market, and how best to present the strongest appeals, bolstered with secondary appeals. Assume that the problem is one special group of dresses at Belk's Department Store. The dresses, according to information supplied by the store manager, were made to sell at $14.95 but are on sale Friday and Saturday at $10.29. They're spring dresses, in a wide variety of light and colorful spring fabrics in ten different styles—all conforming to this year's fashion. Materials include voiles, piques, wash'n wear cotton prints, and Japanese silk.

THE LEAD

The first step is to write a lead that compels the attention of middle class housewives whose family income is in the range of about $5,000 to $10,000, the housewife, we decided earlier, who is fashion-conscious but who also must be thrifty. Let's start our copy with the following lead:

ANNCR: The bright, new styles on sale at Belk's this weekend will make you feel as fresh and desirable as a breath of spring, and you'll save $4.66 on every one.

CREATING INTEREST

The second step is to arouse her interest in these dresses specifically. The best way is to expand on the lead. The subject of becoming as fresh and desirable as a breath of spring has already interested her to the point that you have her attention. Expand on that idea. Get her into the picture; paint a beautiful picture of your prospect enjoying the benefits.

ANNCR: You'll love the exquisite styling, comfortable fit, and fashion-rightness when you see and try them on. You'll marvel at how the light, bright, fabrics make you feel as fresh and desirable as a breath of spring.

DESIRE & CONVICTION

The third step is to create desire. Some writers include a fourth step, which is defined as **conviction**. Most copywriters tend to include the creation of conviction in the process of creating desire, since they go together. Whether you consider it a separate step or not, you recognize that creating conviction in the mind of your prospect is a necessary part of creating desire.

It is a good rule of advertising that the main idea is presented three times. If your main idea can be explained in five words ("Filter, Flavor, Pack or Box"), you'll have no problem in presenting it three times in 60 seconds. If your story is "fresh and desirable as a breath of spring," you still should have no serious problem. But if your story is considerably longer, it would be well to analyze your appeals and reduce your main idea to fewer words. Sometimes it is necessary to settle for two presentations of the main idea.

THE URGE TO ACTION

ANNCR: You'll walk in the wonder of springtime, radiating the essence of loveliness, the object of compliments wherever you wear one of these delightful styles.

Designed to be fashion-right in your life, they're made by a famous name manufacturer to sell for $14.95. With minor imperfections, they're available today and tomorrow at only $10.29 in piques, wash'n wear cotton prints, voiles, and pure Japanese silk. You save $4.66 on every one.

Get into the captivating mood of springtime now. Select the styles you like best today or tomorrow at Belk's—third floor.

CREATING A PROMOTION FOR YOUR CLIENT

Now, let's put together what we've learned about analyzing appeals and organizing copy to present those appeals effectively. Here is a typical small- and medium-market situation. We'll follow it from the beginning to the first piece of copy created for the promotion.

Automobile dealers are the biggest users of local radio advertising. Promotion-minded station managers and sales managers create many varied and effective sales events for auto dealers. Some events, such as end-of-the-model-year sales, necessarily make a strong appeal based on the price factor. Other events are planned especially to avoid a price pitch.

Let's plan and write a piece of copy for Smith Chevrolet, 711 Main Street. The station manager has worked out a plan, a name, a budget, and a schedule to present to Mr. Smith. Now he needs copy which will be recorded on a cassette as part of his presentation to Mr. Smith. The prospective advertiser then will have all the information he needs to make a decision, including the proposed copy platform and the exact sound of the proposed copy.

Here's the story we get from the station manager: Name of the event is "Smith Chevrolet's Tent Sale." I can make arrangements for him to set up two big tents, connecting at the ends, down on that old pasture where Broad Street ends at the bypass. It's easy to get into from all directions and there's plenty of room to park for more customers than he'll have.

The tents are red and white striped to look like a carnival. His wife told my wife's cousin at bridge club last night that he has 58 cars on the floor and he needs to sell every one of 'em yesterday. I looked over his lot this morning and found that he has at least one of every model in the line, six or seven in some models and enough different colors for half a dozen rainbows.

Don't use any dates, just say "it starts tomorrow." Open till 10 every night, and Jim and Jesse and the Virginia Boys will be playing every day. It'll run for a week and we'll remote it several hours a day and again every night, but don't mention that.

The station manager has told us the story as he sees it. What do we do now. Confess to the manager that we don't know what to do or where to start? No! We calmly and methodically start from basic principles and arrive at some useful conclusions.

The most basic question of all is this : "Why would anyone buy a car at a tent sale?" Well, there's no logical reason to buy at a tent sale. They're the same cars that are available today at the dealership. And there won't be any drastically reduced prices. In fact, the purpose of the tent sale is to avoid price appeal and move the merchandise at a better than average markup.

Since there's no logical reason, there must be some illogical reason. Yes, indeed! As they might say in the South Carolina sand hill country, it's some more illogical. But illogical or not, we must know and understand it to write effective copy.

First, Jim and Jesse and the Virginia Boys, a hard-driving country band which sings Bluegrass style and plays rock style at the same time, is an attraction. The fact that the sale is being held in not one but two big tents implies a BIG, BIG, BIG event. In addition, the fact that it's a tent sale says that it's unusual. If it's unusual, a lot of people will go see what it's all about.

So, put them all together—the unusual nature of a tent sale, the two big tents that make it BIG, and the live entertainment—and you have an attraction in itself. Add 58 brand new Chevrolets, at least one of every model in the line, and you have an auto show, which in itself will draw a crowd.

Now it appears that the basic ingredient of the event is excitement. It's an exciting event and a good word-of-mouth campaign would produce a crowd simply because such carryings-on are attractive to a large percentage of the population—especially to the 65 percent middle majority, most of whom lead rather dull and unimaginative lives.

Build a good piece of radio copy to spread the word and emphasize the element of excitement, and we'll have 'em standing in line to get into the tents. After they get in, they'll be part of the mob that is excited by the fine country music with the rock beat. They'll absorb some of the excitement and good feeling that is present throughout the crowd. In a happy, relaxed mood, perhaps equivalent to that attitude generated by a double martini, their inclination to quibble over price will be reduced. They'll be induced by the atmosphere to **want a** new car and want it now. In a sufficient percentage of cases the immediate want will outweigh the desire to shop other dealers and press for the lowest price and highest trade-in allowance.

In the minds of most people in the tents there will be some value attached to the privilege or opportunity to buy an exciting new car under such exciting and unusual circumstances. No one would admit that he would willingly sacrifice 50 or a 100 dollars trade-in allowance for the privilege of buying his new car in a tent, but that situation exists. It is the basis of the success of such a sale. Many prospective car buyers enjoy the atmosphere and the opportunity to do something different to the extent that they are unconsciously willing to pay a substantial indirect price for it. So that answers the first question: "Why would anyone buy a car at a tent sale?"

Now, the next step is to list the appeals and the rationalizations we may want to use in the copy. The appeal is the emotional reason for buying, and the rationalization is the logical reason.

Example:

Today is the day to buy your new Chevrolet at Smith Chevrolet's tremendous Tent Sale.

because

You have a complete selection now that will be depleted tomorrow.

Now let's make a list of both appeals and rationalizations so we'll know what we have to work with when we begin to organize the copy elements.

Appeals

See and inspect all the new Chevys.

Select the model that is made for you.

It's an exciting event you want to see.

Big trade-in allowances.

You can trade fast. Come prepared to drive home a brand new Chevy.

Rationalizations

They're all on display the first day of the sale.

You can compare all the features and prices of every Chevrolet model on the market.

Everybody's going. Big crowd, live entertainment by recording stars direct from Nashville. Every Chevy made this year on display.

Salesmen know what your car is worth; it takes only a minute to have it appraised.

You get action at Smith Chevrolet's Tent Sale. You can get an appraisal of your car and quickly. It takes only a minute at Smith Chevrolet's Tent Sale.

The next step is to decide what type of copy to use. Let's do that now. What is the basic motivation? What is it we want to sell to our listeners? Are we selling cars?

No!

Then what are we selling? For what purpose do we want to motivate our listeners? We're selling the Tent Sale. We want to motivate listeners to go to the Tent Sale. Mr. Smith and his sales staff will sell the cars. It is our job to motivate listeners to go. Forget about selling cars except as part of the attraction of the Tent Sale. Cars are new, and sparkling bright with all the brand new gizmos and gadgets on them. The motivation that will bring prospects into the tents is not any individual gizmo or gadget, but the overall excitement of:

1. Seeing all the great new Chevrolets

2. In the excitement of the BIG, BIG, BIG Tent Sale

3. With the live professional entertainment in the same tent

4. And crowds of excited people coming from miles around

Now, after going through this analysis we can see that excitement is the game, and selling is it's name. What possibilities do we have for selling the excitement of Smith Chevrolet's Tent Sale?

First, for the purpose of further analysis, let's list some requirements that must be considered:

1. The YOU attitude—copy directed to ONE listener, grabbing his attention and interest, telling him about benefits he can get by going to the Tent Sale.

2. Possible ways to present the story are: straight pitch copy; production copy.

3. Tell him the event is exciting, or make him feel the excitement.

4. Make him want to go to the Tent Sale.

Remember that most new ideas are accepted only after the sixth impression. Think about that and remember it. Most new ideas are accepted only after the sixth impression.

Basing our effort, then, on that knowledge, it seems likely that our copy will be more effective if we make the listener feel the excitement rather than merely telling him that the event is exciting. We can make him feel with one impression, but chances are that we can make him believe in no less than six.

Most people can be moved more effectively through their emotions (or feelings) than through logical thought. Even highly-paid executives, who are trained to think logically about their jobs, tend to follow their emotions in personal matters. It is well known that an executive, who is qualified to make complex and responsible decisions affecting hundreds of thousands of dollars of company money, becomes unreasonably disturbed when other executives on the same organizational level receive office furniture that is different from his. Fortune Magazine has reported several times, with bewildered amusement, on that phenomenon.

Consequently, we can see that it is reasonable to use emotional appeals to motivate everyone, executive, housewife, and assembly-line worker alike. In the matter of housing, clothing, recreation, and food, different viewpoints are necessary for effective motivation. Excitement, however, is a universal emotion. It is contagious, as any experienced salesman knows. A good salesman can describe this tent sale to any auto dealer who is not familiar with it and see the dealer catch fire with excitement.

So we'll put excitement into the copy. Rather than depend on a hysterical-type announcer to project excitement, let's put our faith in our own knowledge of copy and production. We'll generate excitement with production, maintain the YOU attitude, and make him want to go to the tent sale.

SOUND:	**CALIOPE, ESTABLISH, FADE AND HOLD UNDER**
ANNCR:	**(TENSE, DRAMATIC DELIVERY) Everybody's talking, everybody's going. Smith Chevrolet's tremendous Tent Sale has 'em all going.**
SOUND:	**EXCITED CROWD NOISE UP AND UNDER.**
ANNCR:	Everyone who likes fine, new cars is going.
MAN:	I hear every model in the Chevrolet line is there.
ANNCR:	Yes, indeed! Fifty-eight gorgeous new Chevrolets. At least one of every model in the line. Three or four colors of some models. A great automobile show in two big tents on the bypass at Broad Street.
WOMAN:	I hear just everybody's going.
ANNCR:	Yes, indeed! Everybody's going to see Smith Chevrolet's tremendous Tent Sale. Fifty-eight sparkling fresh new Chevrolets are waiting for your inspection. Two big tents. Entertainment by Jim and Jesse and the Virginia Boys.
MAN:	I hear it only takes a minute to trade at Smith Chevrolet's Tent Sale.
ANNCR:	Yes, indeed! It only takes a minute. Smith Chevrolet salesmen all know the trade-in value of your car. IT ONLY TAKES a minute to trade and drive home a powerful new Chevrolet.
WOMAN:	Just think. Fifty-eight brand new Chevrolets. At least one of every model.
ANNCR:	Yes, indeed! You'll find one of those sparkling fresh new Chevrolets is right for you. Exactly right. Join the crowd. See the show. At Smith Chevrolet's tremendous Tent Sale, the bypass at Broad Street.
SOUND:	**CALIOPE UP AND OUT.**

BUDGET ALLOCATIONS

In planning or helping a client plan an advertising campaign, it is helpful to know something about his advertising budget and his policy in planning it. In general, retail merchants tend to allocate advertising money in cycles that parallel the store's sales volume. The parallel, however, is not exact; it deviates in a manner calculated to get the most effect from the budget.

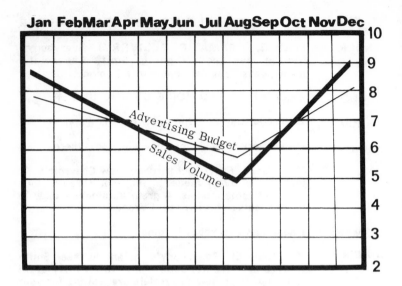

Fig. 4-1. Graph showing seasonal relationship between advertising allocations and sales volume.

The rough chart in Fig. 4-1 indicates a typical budgeting pattern. The sales volume line is not necessarily typical of any business but is exaggerated for the purpose of illustration. The chart shows that the dollar sales volume peaks in December, declining steadily through August, and again climbing to the December peak. A knowledgeable retail store manager has allocated his advertising budget to do more than a proportionate amount of promotion in the weaker months and to compensate for the over-budgeting by under-budgeting in peak months when business will be better because of the season.

Notice carefully that the over and under-budgeting is very slight. This is the pattern that has been found most effective over many years by careful and efficient managers. Many experiments have been conducted in an effort to demonstrate that peak advertising in low-volume months and low advertising in high-volume months is the most effective. It is now generally accepted that such a pattern is an efficient use of the ad budget.

Chapter 5

Adapt Your Power to Your Client

There are many types of copy, each of which is appropriate to a different aim or purpose. To explore some of the possibilities, let's take, as an example, a department store dress department. We'll see how the aim of selling dresses can be handled in different ways.

Institutional copy has two sub-divisions: service and prestige.

The availability of a wide assortment of prestige dresses is the basis for one approach to institutional copy. Assortment (the biggest selection in town) is one aspect of prestige in any type of merchandising. The purpose of this type of copy is to help build an image of the store, in this case an image of prestige dresses in wide variety and the image of this store as the place to go for the finest, most desirable dresses in a wide variety of styles.

Any hack can write "Martin's has the widest variety of smartly fashioned dresses in town." A good copywriter can do considerably better than that in motivating listeners to want some of those dresses. Something like this would come closer to the goal:

ANNCR: (COLD) You'll find the striking Metropolitan Personality in every gorgeous dress you see at Winston-Franklin. Nowhere is it so apparent as in the third floor selection that features fashions the true Metropolite is wearing this spring. Whether you're dancing at the Swan Ball, sitting in the bleachers at the thrilling Iroquois steeplechase, or showing out-of-town guests the wonders of Music City, you know that your dress is perfect for the occasion when you choose from the classic selection at Winston-Franklin. This year it's Metropolitan Personality that sets you apart with the confidence that comes from knowing you're among the style setters. And who could know that Metropolitan Personality better than Winston-Franklin, the pace setter for the style setter. Join the true Metropolites anywhere any time with Metropolitan flair, with Metropolitan style, with Metropolitan confidence. Winston-Franklin, Broadway at 6th, downtown Nashville.

Institutional service copy would take a different approach to the problem, but still would endeavor to build an image of leadership for the store:

ANNCR: (COLD) All the world loves a lover, it is said. But nothing in classic literature has dealt with the problem of today's Metropolite who loves fine dresses. That's where Winston-Franklin comes in. If you love fine dresses, dresses that reflect the true Metropolitan Personality, but can't find the fashion-right creations just right to blend the Metro Personality with your own, take your problem to Winston-Franklin. There you'll find real know-how and super-fast service. If Metro's widest and most distinguished selection of fine dresses for every occasion fails to yield that elusive styling that so perfectly blends your own personality with the pace-setting Metro air, then Winston-Franklin's brilliant and fast-moving designers will create a lush and lovely outfit for you alone. You'll walk in loveliness, radiating the glow and the confidence that springs from true fashion-rightness created just for you. Take all your fashion problems to Winston-Franklin, Broadway at 6th, downtown Nashville.

Promotional copy has two sub-divisions: regular price line and bargain.

Let's assume that Winston-Franklin is now exerting a stronger sales effort in behalf of third-floor dresses. The problem, first, is to produce copy for regular price line dresses, the same dresses treated so prestigiously in the institutional copy.

Notice that the same dresses still have the same prestige, but the sales effort is stronger, aimed at producing more immediate sales. Regular price line copy has something in common with both institutional and bargain copy. It tries for immediate sales, but also establishes preference in the listener's mind, a preference that will remain and be effective next month if she neglects to buy now.

ANNCR: (COLD) You'll make the charm of the Metropolitan Personality your own when you choose from the wide and wonderful selection of fine dresses at Winston-Franklin. Look gay and shining-fresh again, with the glamour and the atmosphere of today's Metropolite. They're vivid and most effective when you slip out of your fur coat. You'll radiate delightful charm wherever you go—at luncheons, little dinners, and evenings when you drop in for a quick one and a floor show. Meticulously selected for the style and the quality that reflect today's Metropolitan Personality, these dashingly modern creations will make "front and center" wherever you happen to be. Join the

Metro style leaders now. Select the flattering style and color that is so right for you. Prices range from $39 to $119. Third floor at Winston-Franklin, Broadway at 6th, downtown Nashville.

Bargain copy emphasizes low price and the necessity of buying now. The season is late and the intrepid buyer of better dresses at Winston-Franklin has discovered that she erred. She bought too many dresses. Now, one well-manicured forefinger is poised quiveringly abaft the panic button as the other hand gropes for a tranquilizer. This copy will help:

ANNCR: (COLD) Here's exciting money-saving news for the truly fashion-conscious woman in Middle Tennessee. Winston-Franklin announces their first and final clearance of better dresses. Now the exciting Metropolitan Personality collection that you may have admired, the silks, the shantungs, the voiles, the crisp and dashing styles—every one of them is on sale. Prices of every one of these gay and shining-fresh fashions are slashed 20 percent. Dresses originally priced at $119 can put sparkling new life into your wardrobe for only $85. The delightful little street dresses that radiate charm and confidence wherever you go are reduced from $39 to only $31. At these big savings you can buy five gorgeous styles of today's style-setting Metropolite for what four would have cost last week. Winston-Franklin's buyer bought too many, now they've got to go. At these prices they will. Better hurry down today for the best selections. Winston-Franklin, Broadway at 6th, downtown Nashville.

Fashion copy explains what is fashionable.

Let us push the button of our own magic time machine now as we move backward into the days before Winston-Franklin's erring buyer threw a whammy on the panic button. Imagine that the season is early and the excitement of Metropolitan Personality has not yet made itself felt outside the rarified atmosphere of the Belle Meade Country Club. It is the job of the copywriter to educate prospects to the desirability of the new style. Here is one way to go about it.

ANNCR: (COLD) The smartest thing in fashion this spring is the Metropolitan Personality, now featured in the Sixth Avenue show windows of Winston-Franklin. Have you noticed? Endless in its slimming flattery, wonderfully suited to your urbane life, the Metropolitan Personality becomes a part of yours. For whatever occasion—a shopping stroll, entertaining at home, or attending an elegant banquet, the Metropolitan Personality puts you out front, out where the pace setters move in splendid confidence and serene charm. The dashing detail of style, the obvious good taste, the gently flowing look, utterly simple in line and detail, mark you as a true Metropolite. When you wear the look of Metropolitan Personality fron Winston-Franklin, you feel like the woman you are. See the brilliant new Metro collection at Winston-Franklin today. Picture yourself walking through life, the Metropolitan Personality blending delightfully with your own, and the designation "front and center" fitting any place you happen to be. Winston-Franklin, Broadway at 6th, downtown Nashville.

Utility copy

Utility copy is concerned with merchandise of a staple character which is bought because of its inherent usefulness rather than because it is a current style or fad. Fashion hardly falls into that category, but for the purpose of illustration let's continue our assistance to Winston-Franklin's harried third-floor management. (Notice that construction copy technique is combined with this.)

ANNCR: (COLD) If you still think of a house dress as any ol' dress to wear around the house, wake up! Quick, dash down to Winston-Franklin and see what they have for you. Vivid new slack suits, designed like a dream and created in striking hard-finish fabrics to hold their shape and flatter yours, await your pleasure. Pleasure is what they bring you with their breathtaking smartness and rugged construction. Every seam is double-stitched; every pocket bar-stitched, and every belt-loop built to last. No matter how you bend, stoop, or stretch in cleaning, cooking, vacuuming, or playing, you can have the confidence that comes from knowing you're dressed for the occasion, the Metropolitan Personality blending stunningly with your own. Tailored in the always appropriate tapered style, the slacks will be just as good next year as they are today. The trim, tailored blouses are always fashion-right and flattering. Both are right at home in the supermarket, on the beach, or driving the kids to school. Best of all, the striking colors will still be strong and clear after a year of hard washing and wearing. If it's a house dress you need wake up! Go to Winston-Franklin, third floor, today, and choose the modern house dress—tapered slacks and tailored blouse. Winston-Franklin, Broadway at 6th, downtown Nashville.

Reason-why copy

Good for almost anything, reason-why copy presents clearly logical reasons why the prospect should buy. It is used most effectively following an emotional appeal. The rule is: first emotionalize, then rationalize.

Let's move down to the first floor annex, now, and offer our copywriting assistance to the store's major appliance buyer. He has just unloaded a big shipment of fine kitchen ranges. He gives us the specifications.

Ajax brand

42 inches wide

24 inches deep

Pushbutton electric model with "settings for everything"

Timers to turn individual burners on and off

Big work space on the porcelain enamel top

Two ovens with separate controls

Five colors: white, avacado green, coral, Georgia peach, shocking pink

Mr. Buyer says he's already tired of looking at 'em. He wants to move 'em out. We take notes, sit down to our trusty typewriter and turn out copy that will leap out and push buttons inside the listener, making her react, making her believe, making her buy.

ANNCR: (COLD) Sooner or later you'll replace that old kitchen range with a new range, a modern range, an automatic electric range that will turn itself on and off while you're out of the kitchen, or while you're out of the house. You don't have to wait. The space-age Ajax range is here today. See it in a rainbow of five tasteful colors at Winston-Franklin now. See how the big, big, worktop gives you an abundance of working room, room to work your kitchen magic on the most complex dishes, leaving you room to spare. This is a big range, 42 by 24 inches, a luxurious range that puts you in command of the most exciting, most satisfying capabilities ever found in a kitchen. You can roast a big tom turkey in one oven and bake a delicate cake in the other at the same time. What's more you can set the automatic timers for both ovens and each range-top burner. Go shopping, play bridge, drive out to the club, anywhere you need to be. This marvelous space-age range does your thinking for you. It turns itself on, does the cooking you instruct it to do, then turns itself off. With the luxurious new automatic Ajax range you're in total command of your kitchen—even when you're out of the house. **The price tag on each of the fashion-right colors is only $299. Sooner or later you'll have one like it. Why not now? Select the color that fits your kitchen today, at Winston-Franklin, Broadway at 6th, downtown Nashville.**

Human-interest copy can be classified into four types:

1. Humorous copy   3. Story copy

2. Fear copy   4. Predicament copy

Fear copy is generally unsuited to the purposes of local radio advertising, so let's discount that type and forget it. The other three types many times are combined into one 60-second production.

Production copy, itself, often indicates a story of some kind; the story is often based on a predicament, and quite often the predicament is humorous. None of these factors is necessary to production, but one or more of them usually goes into production copy.

Assuming that Mr. Buyer could use further help in moving those big, luxurious, fashion-colored ranges off the floor, let us put our shoulder to the Ajax wheel and push. What we want to push is the "hot button" of listeners who are prospects for kitchen ranges. Again we'll try to write copy that will leap out, grab the listener, and push buttons inside her, to make her react, make her believe, make her buy.

SOUND: **PHONE RING**

BETTY: **Hello?**

MARGE: **Oh, Betty, I know you're planning to have Bob's boss over for dinner tonight, but something has just come up at the club and we've just got to have a short committee meeting this afternoon. Could you possibly get away from the kitchen for a few minutes. We've just got to meet.**

BETTY: **Why, sure Marge. Any time. Just say when.**

MARGE: **The earliest we can make it is 2:30, Betty, and the meeting will last at least half an hour. Can you stay that long away from your cooking?**

BETTY: **Sure. I can stay as long as necessary. Didn't I tell you? I've got a new Ajax range. I just put my dinner on the burners, and in the two ovens, set the timers, and forget it. Everything is turned on at the right time and off at the right time. All burners and both ovens are on individual timers.**

MARGE: That's the kind of range a committee member needs for sure. What kind is it?

BETTY: It's the new Ajax. That's the new one—a big, luxurious range. It looks great in my kitchen. I picked the avacado green, but they come in four other colors including white to go with any kitchen decor. Why not get one for yourself, Marge? Every committee member needs one.

Notice that none of this example copy is written to be copied and used for any specific local situation. The Metropolitan Personality is especially written to preclude copying. There is no such style. It is merely an adaptation for illustrative purposes of what Lord & Taylor promoted many years ago as the New York Personality. Except for New York and Paris, and possibly Los Angeles, no city has a personality strong enough to influence general fashion trends. While Nashville is a style center for stage costumes, the proclivity does not extend to street clothes. However, in late 1969, Levy's, a prestige men's store, began to promote the Nashville "Look."

There are several points to be studied in connection with this example copy. First, remember that it is not written to solve a specific problem, but merely to show examples of techniques. While it is above the usual station average, it is not necessarily right for any advertiser. It is right to illustrate some specific principles. Other principles, techniques, and good practices have been ignored for the moment.

ANALYSIS OF PRECEDING COPY EXAMPLES

Institutional, prestige assortment

The lead is weak. A far better lead should be contrived for actual airing. The prospect—quite different from Mrs. Housewife who's looking for a bargain in $14.95 dresses—is among the social elite and social climbers who habitually attend the top social events where wives and daughters of executives and professional men get their kicks by subtly outclassing their friends. Mention of specific events points the copy directly at the prospects.

Mrs Fourteen Ninety-Five Housewife knows it is not directed at her. It puts the prospect in the picture, painting a beautiful vision of her confidence and enjoyment that will come with the wearing of Metropolitan Personality fashions. It departs from traditional institutional advertising (which has a long history in print media) in that it closes with a definite urge to action. It takes only about three seconds to ask the prospect to buy. Why let the opportunity go to waste. Try for a sale every time. As salesmen know, you don't get the order unless you ask for it.

While most radio advertising is directed to the middle majority, it is not unreasonable to aim at the higher economic level when programming is suitable. The Radio Advertising Bureau reports that in the $15,000 and over group, about 35 percent are heavily exposed to radio compared to about 17 percent heavily exposed to TV. Add to this the findings of Daniel Starch & Staff that fewer than one-third of women readers read as much as 50 percent of a full-page department store ad and the opportunities for professional radio advertising techniques are apparent.

Institutional, service

The lead is a little weak, but the subject of love is a strong attraction for that part of the population known to wear dresses. Basis of the pitch is the assurance that Winston-Franklin can solve the prospect's fashion problems. Again the prospect is painted right into the picture, showing her enjoying the service. The same type of copy can be used for almost anything—automobiles, home building, lawn mowers, or bakeries.

Promotional copy, regular price line

The lead is not bad, but not as strong as it could be. The advice to "Look gay and shining-fresh again" gets the prospect right into the picture and she's still there as we tell her "They're vivid and most effective when you slip out of your fur coat." She's still there, anticipating further enjoyment, as we paint in a vision of her radiating charm here and there. The word "dashingly" dabs in a brilliant spot of color that perhaps makes her see herself in a new and more exciting light. The suggestion that she join the Metro style leaders is as welcome as a diamond necklace. That's exactly what she wants to do.

Notice that the department (third floor) is specified. Designation of location is a highly desirable function of copy whenever there is any doubt whatever as to where the advertised merchandise is to be found. In some situations it is desirable to describe the location of the store, such as "Winston-Franklin, Green Hills Shopping Center" or "Sherbles Art Gallery, on West End Avenue between 17th and 18th."

Some astute station managers work out arrangements to cross plug clients in describing store locations. "On Main Street next door to Johnson Furniture Co." reciprocates for "On Main Street next door to Jean's Flower Shop."

Bargain copy

Notice how the tone of the copy is changing through the series, and now has reached the peak of selling effort consistent with the character of the store. It starts off by stressing money-saving news. The word "announce" is one of the best words you can use in a lead, when it is appropriate. Sentences are short and punchy. They're punchy **because** they're short. There's power and an air of urgency going into the announcer's delivery because of the short sentences.

At the same time, the prospect is still being painted into a breath-taking vision of loveliness where she radiates charm and confidence as she moves in subtle ways to outclass her friends. The comparison of value, showing that she can buy five for the original price of four adds to believability. It is specific. The flat statement that all dresses are reduced 20 percent is also specific and adds to believability. The explanation that the buyer bought too many is a plausible explanation of the reason for price slashing.

Fashion copy

Devoted to explaining what is fashionable, the copy starts off with an excellent move by stating that "the smartest thing in fashion this spring is..." The question "Have you noticed?" gets the prospect into the picture immediately, starts her thinking. The next sentence paints her into the picture, explaining how the new style can benefit her.

We depart from traditional fashion copy by including an urge to action. It takes only about three seconds and may make the difference in the minds of some prospects who hadn't really planned to go downtown today, but now change their minds.

Utility copy

The example is a little far-fetched but is used to follow through on the same basic theme. Wide utility is a strong selling point and construction is described in some detail as to seams, bar-stitching, etc. At the same time beauty and glamour is emphasized as an additional benefit, which in the final analysis may be the principal benefit in the mind of the prospect. There is also a reason-why technique used in this example, as there is in most good copy.

Reason-why copy

The lead is good. It makes a statement predicting that the listener is going to do something. It may provoke disagreement but it gets attention. Disagreement is not the belligerent type that is disastrous to the sale, but rather skepticism. First, the copy goes about painting a beautiful picture of the prospect using the Ajax range (emotionalizing), then switches to logical reasons why (rationalizing) it is desirable. It's big, luxurious, can roast a turkey and bake a cake at the same time. Automatic timers leave you free to go, etc. Other emotional motivaters are slipped in easily: "Puts you in command...." "You're in total command...."

Human interest copy

For some writers the dialogue type of copy is the easiest and fastest to write. Others find that it presents almost insurmountable difficulties in imagining realistic conversation.

A tip may be in order in that regard. Realistic conversation for purposes of any form of show business actually must be slightly exaggerated. Just as an announcer must exaggerate his diction and his emphasis on a station break to make it sound natural to listeners, dialogue must be forced a little bit to make your point.

Here, in dialogue copy, is where you can take complete advantage of your listener's imagination. Any situation that you can visualize can be created on the screen of your prospect's mind. It can be humorous, impossible, set in a purple grotto on the planet Jupiter, or as down-to-earth as a mother screaming at a child to hush so she can continue her phone conversation.

This example is extremly simple but gets across the selling points and the appeal of the new Ajax range more effectively than one-announcer copy can. You can incorporate various types of copy into human interest or dialogue copy. You can use dialogue for institutional, bargain, fashion, utility, reason-why, construction, testimonial, endorsement—anything you can do with straight pitch copy. You'll find many examples in Chapter 13.

Story copy

Here is a separate note on story copy, one of the classifications of human interest copy. Suitable for a friendly, easy-going disc jockey, pure story copy can be effective when both the story and the delivery are good. On the basis of what you know about good copy, evaluate this:

ANNCR: (COLD) My favorite person at the moment is Princess Laughing Water, an Indian lady I met at the Sportsmen's Show last week. She curled up in a corner, grimly chewing on a piece of leather. Seems it's an old Indian custom—a squaw's way of making sure her husband's shoes will be soft and comfortable. Immediately I invited her down to McCreery's men's store. She felt the Jarman shoes, marveled at their softness, then gazed reverently at the shoe buyer and said: "He must have hundreds of wives to chew his shoes." If you're a wife, if you're just as interested in your husband's comfort, but don't want to go as far as Princess Laughing Water, let Jarman's extra-comfortable shoes save all that wear and tear on your jaws—at the same time saving your husband's feet from corns and blisters. If you're a man, if you want your shoes to feel as comfortable as moccasins, then McCreery's Jarman shoes are the shoes for you. Dozens of New Spring fashions are ready now. See them today! McCreery's, Fifth Avenue at 34th.

Good radio copy? Yes. It's also good newspaper copy. Written in the 1930s it was published in the New York Times. Adapted for radio by the change of a couple of words, it's still good copy. It is effective because people are interested in people. When a listenable disc jockey says in a believable manner: "My favorite person at the moment is...." almost everyone tends to be curious. The story goes on to illustrate how extremely soft leather can get that way, then compares Jarman shoe leather favorably. The suggestion "if you want your shoes to feel as comfortable as moccasins," gets every man in an agreeable mood because no one can admit that he doesn't want shoes that are as comfortable as moccasins.

This is good, effective copy, edited to perfection. There are no surplus words in it. The main idea—soft and comfortable—is presented three times, although it is less precise the second time. For the right disc jockey the lead is effective, the story is interesting, the motivation effective. If you have the opportunity to write for live disc jockey delivery, this technique can be helpful.

Chapter 6

Power Through Production

In general, production copy is by far the most productive. If your station has facilities and talent for handling production satisfactorily, consider production for every spot or campaign you write. Almost anything can be given more impact with production techniques. Using a range of possibilities from simple dialogue to five voices and eight sound effects, you can add attention, value, emotion, and impact almost as easily as you write a good straight-pitch spot.

The possibilities of production are endless. They cannot be classified and catalogued precisely, but some analysis is possible. From analysis comes guidelines for your efforts in production.

HOW TO EVALUATE YOUR PROBLEM

When you're faced with a copywriting problem, first weigh the necessities of the client's aim against the necessities of copy. Some of the client's necessities may be:

1. Get on the air at 7:04 AM tomorrow.

2. Client wants it done by the morning man.

3. Client insists on including a list of ten "specials."

4. Copy is to be used on a play-by-play broadcast.

5. Copy is to be used on a remote broadcast from the store.

6. Schedule starts in about 48 hours.

7. Copy is to feature one item, one class of items, or one idea.

Now let's consider those necessities and determine how they influence the direction of our copywriting efforts.

1. If the copy must be on the air at 7:04 tomorrow morning and it is now 4:45, a quick job is necessary. There is no time to get the copy produced even if it were already written. The only feasible course is to write it and put it in the book.

2. If the client has specified that he prefers or demands that the announcer on duty in the early morning air the copy, then the decision is made for you. Write the copy and put it in the book.

3. If the client hasn't learned the difference between newspaper listing and good radio copy and he insists on including eight or ten bargain-priced "specials" in each spot, there is nothing you can do at the moment except write the price list for him and put it in the book.

4. If copy is scheduled for play-by-play broadcast, it brings up a question. Must it be read live from the broadcast booth, or is it mechanically practical to cut away and have taped commercials inserted from the control room? This is a question that must be answered by the persons responsible for the broadcast—the chief engineer, the play-by-play announcer, the station manager. If a cutaway is feasible, then a production commercial may be desirable when other requirements and conditions are suitable.

5. If copy is to be used on a remote broadcast from the client's store, chances are it should be live to convey the impression of immediacy and excitement going on at the store now. If the remote is merely a usual disc jockey show originating in the store rather than the control room, there is no reason to avoid production copy, especially for clients other than the store where the remote originates. As in the case of play-by-play broadcasts, if a cutaway is mechanically feasible, production commercials can be inserted from the station.

6. If your only question involving the feasibility of production is sufficient time to get it done, two days normally is adequate, but that depends on the administrative efficiency of your station's management.

7. If copy is to feature one item, one class of items, or one idea, then it appears that you have an excellent candidate for production.

Next weigh the possibilities of production against the possibilities of a straight pitch. Some advantages of production commercials are:

1. Stronger attention-compelling opening, gaining more listeners; a highly desirable goal

2. Projection of more emotion in dialogue; thus a greater impact (on more listeners)

3. More effective in making a point by contrasting two viewpoints

4. Changing voices, tones, and viewpoints holds attention.

5. In dramatized situations, the listener tends to become involved.

6. Increased emotional content tends to make a deeper, longer-lasting impression.

7. Eliminates or reduces the monotony of a heavy commercial schedule

It is readily apparent that production copy is not only suitable but ideal for local retailers in the absence of any built-in obstacles. Normally, anything that can be said in straight pitch copy can be said more effectively in production copy, assuming the availability of competent talent for recording the copy. A 10-second spot can be done with a sound effect and two voices more effectively than with one voice. Assuming 40 words in a 10-second spot, you could write something like this for one voice:

ANNCR: (COLD) Farm-fresh Grade A eggs are only 59 cents a dozen at Big Star Supermarkets today. Save on eggs and a wide variety of other weekend specials at Big Star. Big Star Supermarkets are located in Green Hills, Madison and Donelson.

Wouldn't it be far more effective to sacrifice a few words and gain impact? You might do it like this:

SOUND: CHINESE GONG

FIRST ANNCR It's smart to be thrifty. Save at Big Star Super markets today. Large farm-fresh Grade A eggs only 59 cents a dozen. Big Star—at Madison, Green Hills and Donelson.

For ol' Bob Smith you might write something like this:

ANNCR: (COLD) Planning a weekend trip? Stop in at Bob Smith's Westside Texaco for a complete check up and summerizing service. You'll drive with more peace of mind. Stop at Bob Smith's Westside Texaco today.

For a more effective effort you might do something like this:

SOUND: **TELEPHONE RING**

1ST ANNCR: Hello?... Call back next week. Can't talk now, just leaving on a weekend trip.

2ND ANNCR: For peace of mind, better stop by Bob Smith's Westside Texaco for complete check up and summerizing service.

It has human interest, suspense, and builds interest before making its one point.

In creating a campaign of 10-second spots you might consider the possibilities of producing a series with a combination of tape and live copy. An effective campaign like this could be created with one tape. Put the identifying sound of the Chinese gong on tape along with the line "It's smart to be thrifty, save at Big Star Supermarkets today." Then use live copy to follow the tape. This offers an endless variety of copy, allowing as many changes of items and prices as may be desirable without the time-consuming work of recording each change. One 3-second tape could be used many times a day for week after week with the distinctive sound signaling the listener that "here's another Big Star bargain."

To do this effectively requires conscientious as well as able men on the board. Men who recognize the necessity of tight production and who have the experience and ability to handle it correctly will open the mike as the tape plays and, listening through the headset, come in tight with absolutely no dead air between tape and live copy. This necessitates auditioning the tape before airing to be sure of the cue. Unless your station has such men who can be depended upon to do it correctly, forget it. Record the entire spot.

Here's a possibility for a production campaign. Pick a theme or setting and build all copy for the client around it.

ANNCR: (COLD) And now we take you to the main intersection in downtown Zilch City on the planet Mars where our man on the street, Joe Bloe, is standing by.

JOE:	(UPCUT).....is Joe Bloe speaking to you from the heart of beautiful downtown Zilch City here on the planet Mars. I'm standing on the corner in front of the Zilch City branch of Fred's Fine Fords. With me is Mr. Gus—what's your name again, sir?
GUS:	(WEIRD MARTIAN ACCENT) Zslpty, Gus Zslpty. I'm from Zslptyville. That's a suburb right out here to the South. Named for my grandfather, you know.
JOE:	Your grandfather...oh, yes, I know him. He drove the first Ford on Mars, didn't he.
GUS:	Yes, yes, he did. Mattera fact he bought it from Fred Fine Fords last week. Dented a fender before he got it home, the old fool.
JOE:	Your grandfather likes that big 327 cubic inch Ford engine, all that get-up-and-go and the big luxury of this year's Ford?
GUS:	Yeah, he's just a young fellow by Mars standards, and you know how young fellows are about powerful pickup at stop lights, and passing power and all that, you know. Makes a man feel like the man he is.
ANNCR:	(STRAIGHT PITCH STYLE) Fred's Fine Fords is offering great trade-in allowances this month. You might shave $12 to $15 a month off your payments. Check it out today at Fred's Fine Fords, Space Avenue at Cloud Nine Boulevard, here in Orlando.

A campaign based on such a space-fantasy theme could be built for Fred's Fine Fords, any automobile dealer, boat dealer, service station, supermarket chain, flying school, drug store or chain, resort hotel, virtually anything. Possibilities are limited only by your imagination and your client's approval.

There are no rigid rules for creating such imaginative material, but here are some helpful ideas:

1. An almost believable character (or more than one) set in a totally unbelievable situation and speaking in a routine matter-of-fact manner. The preceding copy set on the planet Mars is an example of this approach. Bob and Ray are masters of the technique. One touch they polished to perfection is the routine pomposity of the big frog in the tiny puddle—the character of the very small man who occupies perhaps the top position in a nothing situation. His voice conveys the attitude of a self-important shipping clerk who

knows all there is to know about his eight-by-ten foot office. The total knowledge and his condescending attitude to a couple of semi-literate assistants is reflected in his voice as he is interviewed by a man-on-the-street who is reflecting something of the same background in his voice. The type is characterized by a service station attendant, who may be casually asked what it will take to end the Vietnam war and proceeds to give a pompous, thorough, and totally illogical solution. Or by a postal clerk who explains impatiently that it is impossible for the mail to be delivered twice a day because individual mail carriers already work eight hours a day making one delivery on their routes.

2. An impossible character speaking in a routine matter-of-fact manner about impossible situations. Personification—giving the power of speech to an inanimate object such as the Ajax range—is one example of this. Another is a man from Mars agreeing that life on Earth is very enjoyable except that he can't accustom himself to the deplorable habit of shaving every day. It's an unjustified drain on his time to shave his three faces every morning.

3. Thoroughly believable characters set in a completely normal situation and speaking of entirely possible matters in a thoroughly normal manner. Notice that space situations are a natural and will be for many years. Other situations that lend themselves to ready understanding and identification on the part of listeners are:

A. Seasonal sports

B. Family situations

C. Children

D. Telephone conversations

E. Boss-employee relations

F. Boy-girl relations

G. Customer-clerk (or salesman) relations

HOW TO DECIDE ON A THEME FOR YOUR COPY

Production copy can be used as an isolated one-day or one-week campaign for a special promotion; it can be used as a long-range campaign; or it can be used in a schedule including other types of copy—straight pitch and jingles.

To create a campaign of production copy, it can be helpful to tie in the situation theme of all spots. The space theme for Fred's Fine Fords could be carried out for months with many changes of copy, all based on space-fantasy.

It might be desirable to intersperse some straight pitch copy in the campaign as a stabilizing influence to convince some more conservative listeners that Fred's Fine Fords is a serious business after all. Different copy techniques and different attitudes toward the product or the advertiser push different buttons in different listeners. Generally, it is better policy to include some production in every campaign, but where your judgment and imagination indicate that it is feasible, create the entire campaign with production copy.

The Unities

The principle advantage of tying a campaign of production copy to one theme is the obvious but difficult-to-describe benefit that comes from artistic esthetic unity. Novelists and short story writers know that a prime rule of fiction (occasionally broken with spectacular results by John D. MacDonald and other truly great story tellers) is to "observe the unities."

Two of the unities are time and place. A good novel or short story is set in a "unit" of time or space, thereby establishing a frame around the story. A production copy series set in a frame of space-fantasy is cohesive, identifiable, and makes a more effective impact on listeners because of its repetitiveness. A campaign of unconnected production copy, however effective each spot might be, would lose effectiveness in comparison, because the listener's thinking would wander around, following the widely divergent ideas. In the "unitized" concept your listener's thoughts are kept focused inside the framework that you create, insofar as your advertiser is concerned. Like the sun's rays focused through a magnifying glass to a small spot, the concentration on a smaller area multiplies the effectiveness.

The old—and good—rule of moderation in all things applies here, also. Good sense must be applied to evaluating units. For a one-week or weekend campaign promoting a store sale, the subject of the special sale constitutes a unit. There, a schedule of fantasy copy based on space, sports, family situation, and boy-girl relations in rotation would not be unsuitable merely because of the unity rule. A longer, less concentrated campaign can benefit from a series of copy ideas tied to the same situation. Paul Garrison reports that stations received fan mail requesting plays of the automatic transmission company spots. (See Chapter 13.)

In writing production copy, you will find many ways to introduce it in the mood you feel is appropriate. Here are some suggestions:

Single Sound Effects of Many Kinds

Telephone bell

Chinese gong

Other types of gongs and cymbal crashes

Automobile starting

Automobile roaring by

Machine gun

One or two pistol shots

Scream

Hammering

Sawing

Horse running

Running footsteps

Dog barking

Music

Trumpet fanfare

Ensemble fanfare

Drum roll and cymbal crash

Mood music of infinite variety

1) Pop or standard
2) Country
3) R & R
4) String ensemble

5) Familiar melody
6) Polka
7) Marching band
8) Single instruments (one-string guitar, piano, clarinet, etc.)

Voice

Heavy sigh, soap opera style

Complaint

Question

Command

Extremely loud and forceful

Soft whispering tone

Man

Woman

Child

URGE TO ACTION IN PRODUCTION COPY

The rule of closing with an urge to action is honored more in the breech than in the observance when it comes to dialogue copy. This is not necessarily good, but it is prevalent in today's radio advertising. The fact that it is prevalent does not make it good.

There is some reason for the modification. It is acceptable in some situations as a compromise in which another desirable result may be accomplished. When such copy is produced by agencies, it usually is for a branded product. Purpose of the agency is to create an image and to build awareness of the product.

Martin Hollinger, media director, BBD&O, Atlanta, points out that when awareness is high as a result of advertising, sales can be expected to rise in proportion. The agency's problem, and your problem as a local copywriter, are not the same. Usually, your copy will be written for the purpose of promoting the immediate sale of specific merchandise ranging from automobiles to ladies panties. Awareness of automobile dealers, department stores, supermarket chains, and furniture stores in small and medium markets is likely to exist almost 100 percent without your help.

While there are many modifications to this principle, usually your goal is to make your listeners want to buy specific merchandise at a specific store rather than to make them aware of a brand name. Consequently, an urge to action is far more valuable to your local advertiser than it is to a national advertiser whose product can be bought in many local stores.

Except for blitz campaigns for tires and occasional other items, the selling pattern of national products is quite leisurely compared to the hard-selling promotions of your local clients. A national advertiser may view a 13-week schedule as a short, hard-hitting campaign to build image and brand recognition or awareness.

Your local client wants action this week. His image is already established. Customer awareness is almost 100 percent. His advertising goal is to bring customers into his store now, today. He can't wait 13 weeks to build recognition of this week's bargains and then wait another month for a research department to analyze the figures. He sees the results of this week's advertising in this week's sales figures.

You must be constantly aware that those sales figures (which you never see) are the only valid measurement of copy quality. Your copy may be beautiful; it may draw raves from the client and his wife; it may be funny enough to break up your mother-in-law; but the key question is this: does it increase sales?

Joseph Stone, president, Berger Stone & Partners, a New York advertising agency, in speaking to the American Advertising Federation convention in Jacksonville, Fla., April 25, 1969, said it this way: "...Be different while making the point you must make to make sales, not while making a useless point only because it lets you be different."

"Don't kid yourself with the great cliche which each year pours billions down the advertising drain, "Stone told the gathering of advertising pros. "That cliche is the great alibi line which reminds me of what happened to Mary L.," he said. "She was young, beautiful, and virginal, till one day sex came into her life. And for the ensuing weeks she was squired by some of the most desirable boys in town.

When her mother guessed what was going on, she told the glowing girl, "If you keep this up, no boy will ever make you his wife."

"Maybe not," said the girl, "But they'll sure talk about me."

Continuing on the same subject, Stone said, "No wiser than Mary L, is the advertiser who says, 'Well, at least it gets attention. At least they'll talk about me.'"

"Don't kid yourself! It is hard to get attention these days. It is hard to deliver a standout message. It is hard to achieve a unique image. But it's not that hard, not so hard that you have to neglect the basic reason why you're advertising in the first place," the agency executive noted.

SOME EXAMPLES OF SIMPLE SOUND EFFECT LEADS

SOUND: **WOMAN'S TERRIFIED SCREAM**

ANNCR: **Oh, shut up, Myrtle, I'm not going to take your new Shocking Pink Ajax range. I just want to look at it. Oooooh, just look at those timers......**

SOUND: **HAMMERING**

WOMAN: **Hurry, Bill, get that mess out of the kitchen; I'm expecting the girls for bridge club any minute.**

BILL: **You're gonna play bridge in the kitchen? This I gotta see.**

WOMAN: **No, silly, we're not going to play bridge in the kitchen, but I want to show the girls my new Shocking Pink Ajax range.**

SOUND: **SAWING (ESTABLISH, FADE AND HOLD UNDER AT MEDIUM LEVEL)**

WOMAN: **Whatcha doin' Bill? (sexy, insinuating manner)**

BILL: **(bored) Oh, I'm building that magazine rack I told you about. Why?**

WOMAN: **(same sexy manner) Oh, ummmm hmmmmm, etc etc. It's nice. How much longer will you be?**

BILL: **Maybe a couple of hours. Why aren't you in the kitchen. I thought you were cooking dinner.**

WOMAN: **Oh, I am, Bill. I am. We're having a standing roast and French cut beans almandine, and creamed potatoes and upside down cake, and fresh hot rolls, and...**

BILL: **Oh, sure. And it's all cooking itself while you're down here in the basement.**

WOMAN:	Yes, honey. That's the way I cook since you bought me that marvelous new Ajax range from Winston-Franklin.
SOUND:	**HORSE RUNNING**
MAN:	(Panting, straining) Come on Big Mack's Whirling Pink Shadow the Fourth. Come on boy. Go, go, go. Gotta win this race and get home. Roast beef for dinner and dinner's always on time since I bought her that new...
SOUND:	**RUNNING FOOTSTEPS**
MAN:	(Panting, straining) Gotta get home for dinner. Meals are always on time now since I got her that new Ajax range.
SOUND:	**DOG BARKING**
MAN:	Move over, Rover, I'm living with you now. Ever since I told her we're getting power ashtrays for the boat.
SOUND:	**SINGLE BARK**
MAN:	Yeah, she wants to let real necessities wait and spend our money on luxuries like that new Ajax range she saw over at Bob and Betty's. Just because it has a timer for both ovens and each burner and comes in five fashion-right colors.....
SOUND:	**TRUMPET FANFARE**
ANNCR:	Winston-Franklin announces....
SOUND:	**ENSEMBLE FANFARE**
ANNCR:	Winston-Franklin's first and final clearance starts tomorrow.
ANNCR:	(COLD) It's coming tomorrow!
SOUND:	**DRUM ROLL AND CYMBAL CRASH**
ANNCR:	Winston-Franklin's first and final clearance sale.

SOUND:	**FANFARE**
ANNCR:	It starts tomorrow.
SOUND:	**DRUM ROLL UNDER AND BUILDING TO CYMBAL CRASH**
ANNCR:	Winston-Franklin's first and final clearance sale.
SOUND:	**UP FULL FOR CYMBAL CRASH**
ANNCR:	Now, at the nation's lowest prices, you can fill your wardrobe with glamour. Today, while the selection is complete, etc....

SOUND:	**SINGLE VIOLIN PLAYING SUPER SWEET OR GYPSY TYPE MUSIC UP AND UNDER**
MAN:	(heavy soap opera sigh) Darling, I promise you happiness...forever!
WOMAN:	Oh, it's all so wonderful. A girl couldn't possibly want any more. But there is one thing.
MAN:	What's that, darling. What more can I do to make you happy.
WOMAN:	I'd be the happiest girl in the world if I just had one of those new Ajax ranges from Winston-Franklin.

SOUND:	**AUTOMOBILE STARTING AND RUNNING**
WOMAN:	I like your new car, Joe.
SOUND:	**AUTOMOBILE ROARING BY**
WOMAN:	There goes Joe in his new Widget 8.

SOUND:	**WEIRD SPACE-CRAFT TYPE WAILING OR WHINING, HIGH-PITCHED AND FLUCTUATING**
MARTIAN:	(martian accent) Earth Landing One to Mars Control. Come in please.
CONTROL:	Mars control. Go ahead Earth Landing One.
MARTIAN:	Today we observed Earthlings in native habitat. In Orlando many of them qued up at a place known on Earth as Fred's Fine Fords.

CONTROL: Clarify please. What is que?

MARTIAN: Que is a long line of Earthlings. They were lined up at Fred's Fine Fords for bargain prices on air conditioned Fords.

CONTROL: Clarify please. What is Ford?

For some copy you'll want a hard-charging attitude from the first sound to the last. For others you'll find that a more leisurely pace makes the impression you're trying for.

The Big Star example is a hard-charger. The award-winning Music To Watch Girls By for Pepsi-Cola is just the opposite. First the music is up full, then fades for the announcer to intone in his best emcee style that he's presenting girl-watching music. Music is again brought up full for 15 seconds as though the show were getting underway or an album is being programmed. Then it fades and is held under for about 10 seconds of alliterative copy dealing with the girls girl watchers watch. Then the music is brought up full for 15 seconds, faded and held under for about five seconds of copy, then brought up full four seconds to the conclusion.

More than half the 60-second time is devoted to music. Perhaps the greatest effectiveness of this production is in the integration of copy with music. First the music, bright, attractive and modern, is established. Then the listener hears what appears to be an introduction to a music segment. The title "Music To Watch Girls By" is so provocative that it grabs the attention of everyone, young and old, especially girls, who might reasonably have some interest in the subject of girl watching. The music is brought up again as though the show is going to proceed. Then, as the listener is lulled into appreciation of music supposed to be especially good for girl watching and wondering why that is so, he is hooked again.

After the main idea is established and supported by the statement that Pepsi-Cola is the only, etc... the listener is returned to the bright attractive music thinking about the main idea. Then after 15 seconds the main idea is brought out and dropped into his lap the second time. All in a pleasant, extremely relaxed mood. It gets across the main idea, which is that the girls girl watchers watch drink diet Pepsi-Cola.

It is all there in that one sentence. It cannot be said better. It cannot be said at all in fewer words. There is a strong association with a pleasureful feeling generated by the music, and perhaps an anticipation of girl watching activities on the part of both the watcher and the watched; also a pleasureful result.

Few commercial productions can afford to take such a leisurely approach, but when the job can be done that way, do it. The slack in content can be handled with words as well as music. Don't let the barrier of tradition keep you from producing the most effective commercials you know how. Tradition in all matters is based on two factors: one is effectiveness that has been proven over and over. The other is simply that no one has yet thought of or had the opportunity to use a better idea.

Another way to impress your main idea more effectively than with straight pitch copy is to personify your product or store. Depending on your own imagination, on the impression you're trying to convey and the attitude of your client, you can treat the personification with the utmost dignity, with easy relaxed friendliness, an amused tolerance, or with ridiculous exaggeration.

You can use the personification technique in many different ways. In the case of Winston-Franklin's Ajax range you might handle it something like this:

AJAX: **(MANNER OF POMPOUS BOREDOM) Well (heavy sigh) I'd really like to go home with you and brighten up your kitchen with one of my five fashion-right colors, and provide my big 24 X 42 inch work top for you. But...well...you see, ma'm...(heavy sigh) I'm not sure we'd be compatible.**

HOUSE-WIFE: **What do you mean compatible? Winston-Franklin is advertising big luxurious Ajax ranges in five delightful fashion-right colors. And you're a big, luxurious Ajax range in shocking pink with all that wonderful working room on top. I want you, Ajax, and I'm going to have Winston-Franklin deliver you to my kitchen today.**

AJAX: **Uh...well...you see, ma'm (heavy sigh) I come from a long line of luxury ranges and appliances. My family goes into only the best kitchens, kitchens of women who know and appreciate the best, women who are accustomed to having their neighbors envy their modern, efficient, and convenient kitchens.**

HOUSE-WIFE: **Why, Ajax! ...You're just perfect for my kitchen. I'm going to have Winston-Franklin deliver you today.**

AJAX: **(sigh) Oh...all right...You seem like a nice enough type. (sigh)...But I usually ask for references.**

Incomplete as it is, this illustrates one of many possibilities of personification. You could use the same technique to personify the Winston-Franklin Store, a drive-in restaurant with 27 varieties of sandwiches, a lawn mower, an automobile, an airplane, a department store itself, a residence, anything.

You can make your points and convey the impression you want about the store or product in a stronger manner when you use contrasting viewpoints with a conflict. The conflict of wills or of viewpoints loads human interest into the copy and continues to hold the interest you created with your lead. At the same time you are developing desire and conviction in the minds of your listeners. Not merely because you're using production copy with greater attention value, but because you're using your knowledge of the 4-step motivational process to produce highly effective copy. This is copy that refuses to lie soggy in the bowl. It snaps, crackles and pops, talking to the prospect, getting him involved mentally and emotionally, leaping out to push buttons inside him to make him react, make him believe, make him buy.

MAKE MAXIMUM USE OF TALENT AVAILABLE TO YOU

Too often, stations overlook widely effective production possibilities because of a failure to evaluate all talent on the staff. It is a tendency of station managers, who understandably must devote most of their concern to details of keeping sales up and costs down, to overlook extroverted manifestations of talent as only useless horseplay.

A manager—or staff copywriter—would be well advised to evaluate all such horseplay from the viewpoint of usefulness in production commercials. A disc jockey who has one or more character voices could (and probably gladly would!) put his ability to work in production for the benefit of advertisers. A staff salesman who may come out with an exaggerated Southern accent or Brooklyn dialect might be happy to contribute a few minutes work now and then to bringing good production copy to life. A fulltime copywriter who is unqualified for general air work may come up with a conversational or even a character voice that can be used in combination with professional voices.

A staff copywriter is in an excellent position to coordinate all the currently unused talent possibilities simply by asking persons who appear to have some ability if they would be willing to help in a production. After gaining assent of the talent, the copy can be written to utilize whatever is available.

A copywriter who can contribute his own voice to a minor role in production is one step ahead of a copywriter who cannot.

Imaginative copy production is mostly the responsibility of the copywriter, whether that copywriter is a station manager, salesman, or a fulltime writer. In considering production possibilities, the effective copywriter continually looks for ways to be different—not just for the sake of being different, but for the purpose of being more effective, of attracting more listeners, creating a greater impact on them, to make them react, make them believe, make them buy.

Being different is not a goal in itself. As Joseph Stone remarked to his audience at the American Advertising Federation convention in Jacksonville:

"Different, today, is a man who walks down the street with flair pants with an abstract print.

"Different also is a man who walks down the street with no pants."

"More different is a man who walks down the street stark naked."

"So we see there's **smart** different and **dumb** different.

"There's eye-catching different.

"Breath-catching different.

"And cold catching different"

One often overlooked source of help in that direction is the chief engineer, or perhaps a combo man who has some realistic knowledge of electronics in addition to his question-and-answer ticket that hangs on the wall of the transmitter room. The electronic modification of voices and other sounds offers endless possibilities. Many times the discussion of a desirable result with the chief will bring instant information and cooperation. Other times he may cogitate on the problem for a month and finally decide it could be done, but it would cost too much in time and money. Or he might be able to suggest an alternative route to achieve a different but desirable result. A friendly, relaxed discussion of possibilities is the best way to go about gaining cooperation. Chief engineers are notoriously resistant to insistent demands from the program department.

Here's another example of a far-out fantasy used for a down-to-earth purpose. An echo chamber, which the chief could build from scraps or surplus, would add to its effectiveness:

ANNCR: (COLD) And now we take you to the University of Mars, where our reporter, Joe Bloe is standing by.

JOE: (UPCUT) .....Bloe speaking to you from the office of the Dean of Students at Mars University. Here with me is Dean Johann Sebastian Zilch. Tell me, Dean Zilch, how much damage did the militant students do?

DEAN: (SLIGHTLY MUSHMOUTHED AND SEMI-LITERATE) Well...I mean...you know...there hasn't been no damage since I've been in office.

JOE: (SURPRISED) Oh, I thought that burned drapery and that broken desk and the papers dumped out of the file...

DEAN: Aw...that was all done...you know...I mean...my predecessor. Know what I mean? Like that...you know.

JOE: How long have you been in office, Dean Zilch?

DEAN: Oh, like two hours man, you know. They wouldn't meet our non-negotiable demand and we threw 'em out, y'know?

JOE: And what was that demand, Dean Zilch?

DEAN: Just a big, luxurious, powerful Ford from Fred's Fine Fords. You know Fred's sellin' 'em off at 15 percent off list price this week and...

JOE: Fifteen percent off list for all those big, powerful luxurious Fords? That seems like a perfectly reasonable demand. Anyone can afford one of Fred's Fine Fords at 15 percent off the list price.

DEAN: Naw...you're not with it man. What we want, we want one big, luxurious Ford from Fred's Fine Fords for each student, you know...

JOE: Why, yes, naturally every student wants a big, luxurious Ford for himself. But no university could possibly afford it.

DEAN: Sure, they could do it easy. Just cut out a few faculty teas and like that, you know?

DEAN:	Oh, yes, I see now. Anybody can afford a Ford from Fred's Fine Fords at 15 percent off this week. Just cut out a few faculty teas.....
SOUND:	**FADE LAST LINE FOR**
ANNCR.	Low prices and high trade-ins. Fifteen percent off the sticker price this week. Fred will put you in a fine new Ford, big powerful, and luxurious, at what may be the lowest monthly payment in town. Drive in at Fred's Fine Fords and check it out today.

Here's an example of staff written copy for a local Ford dealer. It was done by WENO, an all-country station licensed to Madison, a Nashville suburb. Notice the strong appeal to the emotional desire for more power.

SOUND:	**JINGLE (customed produced for the client)**
ANNCR:	**(STRONG, DEEP, POWERFUL VOICE, CONVEYING THE IMAGE OF POWER)** The Cobra Ford! Raised in a tough neighborhood...
SOUND:	**ROARING RACE CAR UP AND UNDER**
ANNCR:	Riverside!
SOUND:	**RACING CAR UP AND UNDER**
ANNCR:	Atlanta! Great in competition, yet gentle on a Sunday drive.
SOUND:	**RACING CAR SEGUES TO UP TEMPO MUSIC**
ANNCR:	How about a Cobra his and hers from **Chapman Ford,** the tudor hardtop and sports roof model. You've never seen so much performance per dollar before. The formula is simple. Cobra Ford puts the money in the muzzle and gives you a car born to move.
SOUND:	**MUSIC UP FULL FOR ABOUT HALF A SECOND TO PUNCTUATE, AND UNDER**
ANNCR:	And at Chapman Ford you'll see the nearest thing to a NASCAR stocker that you can bolt a license plate onto. So don't wait. Come on in today to **Chapman Ford, 2730 Lebanon Road,** the last of the little dealers, and drive away in your new Cobra.

Here's an example of testimonial copy written for production. It was produced in a professional recording studio and scheduled on several Nashville stations.

ANNCR: (COLD) Friends, here we are in the kitchen in the home of Kitty Wells, the queen of country music, and Kitty has just taken a giant bottle of Coca-Cola from the refrigerator.

KITTY: It's the new one-way family size bottle, Jim, with the resealable cap. My husband, Johnny Wright, will show you how it works.

JOHNNY: Nothing to it. Just twist the cap off, then you pour a glass of Coke.

SOUND: POURING AND SZZZZZING OF COKE BEING POURED INTO GLASS.

JOHNNY: Then you twist the cap back on, which reseals the bottle.

ANNCR: What does this resealing do, Johnny?

JOHNNY: Keeps the great taste of Coke bright and bubbly till you're thirsty again.

ANNCR: Man, that's a big bottle.

JOHNNY: Big enough for five glasses of Coke over ice. And it's a no-deposit bottle.

ANNCR: The bottle you don't bring back.

KITTY: And it stores so easy. You can stand it up or lay it on its side.

ANNCR: A good point, Kitty. A lot of Coke in a little space. And friends, this convenient new family size bottle of Coca-Cola is now at your favorite store in the Nashville area. Just look for the bright red label on the big bottle with the reseal cap. No deposit; no return.

Notice that the testimonial copy was tightly written and perfectly edited, not left to the whims and unprofessional ideas of the personalities. It is fully professional and effective:

A. The lead has human interest.

B. Interest is created further by the voice of a star and her participation in action. She actually is doing something.

C. Interest is heightened as her husband, Johnny, gets into the act.

D. Interest is further heightened by the action and the sound of pouring. Something is happening, not just talk.

E. Desire is created by "Big enough for five glasses of Coke over ice." Obvious evidence that the big bottle is desirable when lots of Coke is needed.

F. Desire is reinforced by Kitty's last line. "It stores so easy." And by the announcer's restatement "A lot of Coke in a little space."

G. Conviction is aided by having the stars, with their earthy, unprofessional diction, make the selling points. When Kitty Wells says "It stores so easy," her fans, admirers, and respecters believe. When Johnny, prince consort and leader of the Kitty Wells band, says "nothing to it" the same listeners believe.

H. The announcer urges action, tells where to buy it, what to look for, and repeats an idea previously stated another way: "No deposit; no return."

I. The main idea of the giant bottle with the resealable cap is brought out three times.

This is fine copywriting. It violates one cardinal rule of radio copy but one that may be forgiven since the purpose was to conform to the country music image, which has a tradition of its own. The rule, which is discussed later, is this:

Always address your copy to one single listener. Never direct your copy to listeners in the mass, or a group or class of listeners.

Here's a spot written by Joel Morris, executive of the Morris Furniture Store chain in Nashville. Characterized by an agency owner as a serious student of copy, Morris wrote this to give wives ammunition to overcome objections of their husbands.

There are many things that keep wives out of stores, he noted, adding that the objections of husbands are high on the list. "Give them ammunition to overcome their husbands' objections and they're that much closer to the store," the furniture executive declared. Here's the copy:

ANNCR:	(LIVE) And now let's take a look at the secret lives of Helen and Chris.
TAPE	
CHRIS:	(ANGRILY) Helen! Helen, don't you hear me?
HELEN:	I'm sorry. I was reading about the wonderful Frigidaire appliances that Morris Furniture is advertising in the paper.
CHRIS:	Helen, we can't afford a new Frigidaire appliance of any kind right now.
HELEN:	It says right here we can pay as little as seven dollars monthly. We can afford that.
CHRIS:	But we have no down payment.
HELEN:	It says Morris doesn't require a down payment.
CHRIS:	Well, OK. Morris has nine stores. We'll go to the closest store to us and look.

In 35 seconds (including the live intro) this copy:

A. Grabs attention with strong human interest—family argument

B. Presents the advertiser's name three times and the product name twice, about par for copy of this length

C. Successfully overcomes the "can't afford it" objection by making the point that anyone who can afford seven dollars a month can afford new luxury.

The goal of this copy deviates from the theme of this book which is that good copy should "make'em want it." The furniture store executive knows that a substantial market for his merchandise exists behind the wall of objections raised by husbands. His goal here was to help his prospects—wives—overcome some of those objections and get them into the stores.

Here is an example of semi-hidden motivation being used in a type of business that rarely uses radio. Robert G. Fields & Co., a Nashville advertising agency, produced this for Dealy-Rourke, the city's largest employment agency. It's quite different from the client's newspaper advertising which consists almost entirely of job listings. Glamorized listings, to be sure, but still listings. This radio copy is used to supplement the considerable classified space used daily and Sunday. It is a classic example of Elmer Wheeler's advice to salesmen to "get in step with your prospect."

He illustrated the point by telling how a panhandler, sitting on the curb, got up as Wheeler approached and, walking toward him, asked for a dime. It was too much trouble to stop, fumble for a dime and pull it out of his pocket as he was stopped there on the sidewalk, so Wheeler kept walking and the bum got nothing. Another panhandler, Wheeler noted, saw him coming, started walking slowly in the same direction until he was walking side-by-side with Wheeler. When the request for a dime came, it was no trouble for The World's Greatest Salesman to reach into his pocket and pull out a dime as he continued his walk uninterrupted.

This radio copy is in step with the client's overall advertising effort, building an image of possible romance or other goodies that can be involved in a change of jobs. It utilizes the listener's imagination, which is one of radio's greatest advantages, to add depth to a single girl's thoughts about changing jobs. The motivation is well known to everyone. However, it is almost completely ignored by most employers and employment agencies as being something that "we shouldn't talk about." Robert G. Fields came face to face with the spade, recognized it, and stuck the correct label on it. He has done a job that will be remembered. Here's his copy:

TAYLOR: (mumbling and happily singing to himself) Secretaries are hard to find....I'll take the Miss Davis kind...dum de too to dum de, etc.

SOUND: **OFFICE BUZZER**

DAVIS: (through intercom) Yes, Mr. Taylor?

TAYLOR: Miss Davis, I want to congratulate you on the wonderful job you've been going in the department. However, we need two more secretaries.

DAVIS: Yes, Mr. Taylor.

TAYLOR: Now, since you promoted the last two girls this month, how about calling Dealy-Rourke and let's add two more to the staff.

DAVIS: Yes, Mr. Taylor.

TAYLOR: Start'em out around...oh...four hundred dollars, and give'em two weeks vacation this year.

DAVIS: Yes, Mr. Taylor.

TAYLOR: (to himself) mmmmmm....that's the most efficient, good looking woman I've ever seen. Wonder what she'd say if I asked her to marry me.

DAVIS: Yes, Mr. Taylor.

ANNCR: Dealy—Rourke doesn't guarantee a Mr. Taylor in every single secretary's life, but it has been known to happen. See Dealy—Rourke, downtown, West End, Madison, Hundred Oaks, and Green Hills. The match-makers? The career makers!

This copy was used on WSM with a 5-minute weather summary Monday, Wednesday, and Friday at 5:25 PM as thousands of career girls were on their way home from a day in the (perhaps unsatisfactory) office.

Chapter 7

Language as a Power Tool

Some writing seems to snap, crackle and pop with power. Other writing just lies there. Here are some observations about why that is true. Underlying these observations is a warning regarding the use of slang or other nonstandard language in commercial copy. Nonstandard is not, perhaps, the best term, since standards vary among income, social, and age groups. It is not intended to discourage simplified and pointed language that gets your point across effectively.

There is, of course, a place for certain attitudes of language in developing characterization. But it is important to distinguish between developing a hip or clownish character for an actor in your commercial drama and developing that same character for your client's store or merchandise. Because of the progressive attitude and general awareness of radio personnel, it sometimes seems that anyone on whom current colloquialisms are lost is too far out of the mainstream of life to be a prospect. That is not necessarily the case. People respond to words, phrases, voice tones, and sounds in ways that are consistent with their past experience to the same words, phrases, tones and sounds.

Perhaps you recall the story of Pavlov's dog. Pavlov was a psychologist, researching the behavior of animals, including the human animal. Immediately prior to feeding the dog, he rang a bell. Then he presented food to the dog. After several days he observed that the dog began to salivate upon hearing the bell. He then rang the bell several times a day without giving food to the dog every time. The dog salivated upon hearing the bell every time. He was conditioned by the sound of the bell to expect food. When his mind expected food, his body involuntarily prepared for food.

Sounds, words, and phrases activate unthinking habits in humans just as the sound of the bell activated an involuntary habit in the dog, a habit over which the dog had no control and couldn't have stopped if he had tried.

The same words, phrases, accents, and manners of speaking have different emotional effects on different people.

The use of words that may be associated with unpleasantness in the mind of a listener can produce hostility, just as well-chosen music can evoke a pleasant response.

A college president who has just come through a brutal experience at the hands of the hippies and New Left could very well be repelled by the light use of "non-negotiable demand." Consider the differences in these words:

Officer

Policeman

Cop

Fuzz

Pig

Each of the four words is used to refer to the same people. "Policeman" is acceptable to everyone who is acting in good faith. "Cop" is acceptable to virtually everyone, although it infers less than desirable dignity in the view of some. "Fuzz" is unacceptable in serious writing or in the conversation of responsible persons. "Pig" is totally unacceptable to responsible persons under any circumstances. The use of either "Fuzz" or "Pig" in the hearing of a responsible person immediately stimulates a vision of the type of undesirable who would use those words.

It is well for the responsible copywriter to evaluate carefully the use of all such contemporary slang to avoid conveying an impression or building an image that is the opposite of the one he intends. Most of the so-called hippie talk originated among the more irresponsible elements of the Harlem community. Born of irresponsibility, nurtured on rebellion, and matured in street violence, it is peculiarly misplaced in the advertising of respected businesses.

There is a direct parallel between this type of slang and jazz. While jazz has climbed several rungs up the ladder of respectability, it has never completely lived down the circumstances of its birth in New Orleans' red light district. Neither has the general public—and Mrs. Middle Majority Housewife—been able to overlook its primary social sin: nonconformity. The American public can forgive any other sin—murder, rape, robbery, wife beating or gossip. But forgive, forget and accept nonconformity? Never!

There is a distinct difference, however, between **colorful** writing and the simple use of questionable slang. Colorful writing is desirable many times to convey the attitude, impression, or image you want to impress upon your listeners. The two techniques are similar in that **colorful** writing utilizes a nonstandard word or phrase, usually a noun or verb, to add attention-holding interest to an otherwise dull or uninteresting sentence.

For brilliant examples of colorful writing read the novels of John D. MacDonald, half a dozen of which are available at any given time on every good paperback rack. You'll find examples on every page. MacDonald, who is one of the all-time great story tellers, accomplishes the same purposes in his novels that you must accomplish in about 14 lines.

1. He grabs the reader's **attention.**

2. He arouses **interest** in the predicament.

3. He creates **desire** to finish the story.

4. The reader is moved to **action**—finishing the story (and usually buying MacDonald's next novel).

Along the way he adds infinite variety to basically uninteresting details by describing the usual in an unusual way.

When you're tempted to dip into the hip for added interest, first check the possibilities of producing stronger copy by more imaginative use of the English language.

1. Verbs are words that add movement. They cut, run, dash, swim, dip, dive, dash, lash, dance, sparkle, throw, jump, hop, grow, build, drive, and generally jam life into your copy. You can write "Stop in at Belk's when you're downtown. Save on fashion-right dresses for spring." You can put more life and vitality into the same idea by writing "When you're downtown today, dash into Belk's and save on fashion-right...." Or: "**drive** into Belk's parking lot; **hop** into the convenient elevator..."

In another context you might be more graphic in regard to saving.

"Save a potful."

"Save a fistful of cash."

"Save a purseful of cash."

"Buy your new Maverick from Honest John today; save a trunkful of cash."

2. Nouns are words that name something or someone. The better writers of popular magazine articles rarely call anything by its legal name. Substitution of a more informal name for a standard term is the key to most of their color. This particular type of colorful writing is carried to its peak by sports writers who absolutely refuse to call a spade a spade. Instead they refer to a base hit as a bingle, a base lick, a single, etc.

Joseph Stone suggested in his Jacksonville talk to advertising pros that to talk fresh, while the words are still fresh, calls for one part of invention and one part of awareness. As Stone put it to the pros: "In the invention area, your first step is to avoid the heavy, Latin-root, multi-syllable words. Instead, use the short, sharp, crisp, Anglo-saxon words which team up into interesting new combinations.

"Instead of a car with performance talk of a car with 'git.'

"Instead of rugged and durable, say it's 'Built like a battleship, to laugh at time.'

"Instead of maximum so and so, 'top so and so.' Instead of durability, 'they last and last.' For reliability, 'it always works.'

"Put those tiny words into colorful phrases such as 'git-and-run-driver,' 'easy does it,' 'Get a Chevy while it's hot,'" Stone advised.

ABOUT THAT MERCHANDISE

The word merchandise should never be used in an effort to motivate prospects to buy retail merchandise. This is purely a trade word. It has a specific meaning to a merchant. It represents his stock in trade, his inventory investment. To him it has a specific and realistic meaning. But it has no place in retail advertising because retail customers never buy merchandise. They buy dresses, shoes, costume jewelry, hosiery, shirts, building materials, tires, automobiles and pianos.

Webster's Collegiate describes Merchandise as "objects of commerce; wares; goods." Customers go into a store to buy specific items to fill specific needs. Neither the word merchandise nor its meaning relates to a customer's wants or needs. Mrs. M. Majority cannot picture herself wearing merchandise. She cannot imagine merchandise performing any useful function in her home. She cannot visualize herself being any happier, lovelier, healthier, or more fashionable for having bought merchandise. She can, however, easily picture herself wearing a dress, shoes, costume jewelry, and hosiery. She can just as easily picture her husband and sons wearing shirts, underwear, socks, and walking shorts. The professional copy writer uses words that **relate to human needs and wants**, rather than trade words without specific meaning to retail customers.

ABOUT THOSE NEEDS

It is a common experience to hear copy on otherwise good stations suggesting "For all your back-to-school needs go to Belk's." "For all your fertilizer needs... For all your kitchenware needs... For all your hardware needs..." The word "needs" in this context is as nebulous as "merchandise" and just as useless. It has no direct relation to human needs and wants. Forget it!

If you're writing copy for hardware, give an accurate description of **which** hardware and relate it to **specific** needs and wants. There's builder's hardware for home improvement; nuts, bolts and related hardware for home repairs; electrical supplies for repairs, expansion, and improvement; plumbing hardware, kitchen hardware, and other kinds of hardware.

One store may carry them all, plus much more. But the word "needs" does not relate specifically to any of them. It paints no picture of benefits. It directs no attention to possible benefits the prospect could enjoy by buying. It is a poor word. It has no motivating power. It does nothing to make the prospect want anything. Forget it. Wipe it out of your copywriting vocabulary!

ABOUT THAT ADDRESS

The purpose of your copy is two-fold: to inform, and to motivate on the basis of that information. Good copy practice requires that you use enough words to inform your prospects as completely as practicable, but not one word more. If your spot rate is $3 and you average 150 words per minute, each word is costing your client two cents. In larger markets where the rate may be $60, the cost is 40 cents a word.

So what, a novice asks. The client is not buying words. He's buying impressions, spots, or selling messages. In one sense, yes. Regardless of words, singly or collectively, the client's interest is in the message. In the same sense, his interest is in the suit he buys, not in the individual threads from which the material is woven. But beware selling that client a suit with rotten threads in the material.

Let's consider the job of editing before we proceed further. Editing is a career in itself, but a copywriter, especially in a radio station, usually must edit his own copy. Writing is one ability; editing is another. Most writers are not good editors, even when they're good writers. Thomas Wolfe is said to have been one of the greatest novelists of this century. Yet, without an editor operating independently of Wolfe, his work would not have been publishable. Trade talk is that Wolfe, a prolific writer, to say the least, wrote by the pound. The editor eliminated much of the material, reorganized some of what was left, and put it into shape much like a farmer shaking down and shaping up a bag of grain. The result is a shelf of great novels.

In print media a good editor is harder to find than a good writer because it is a much more exacting job. It is exacting because it requires detailed judgment about each individual word, each suffix, each affix, comma, semicolon, and ellipse. A good radio copy editor gets his client more sell per dollar, more motivation in 60 seconds than the neophyte who thinks a word here and a word there is unimportant.

This is why careful editing and elimination of every unnecessary word is important. Good editing is one of the sharpest tools in the professional copywriter's bag. Eliminate one unnecessary word at the end and you may be able to insert one motivating word in the middle. Unnecessary words are those which neither inform nor motivate and which add nothing to the grammatical completeness.

In most small and medium markets the name of the state in which the station and the advertisers are located comes within that category. There is some variety of opinion about the desirability of including the state name. One view is that people love to hear the complete address with the town and state. There is another view that station management (including department heads with delegated responsibility) is more competent to decide such matters. There is no doubt that good practice in writing dictates the elimination of the state name when it can be done with no diminution of clarity. The style books of both AP and UPI specify elimination of the state designation after any city when, in the judgment of the writer, no loss of clarity will result. Continually informing your listeners that your station and advertisers are located in "Midville, Texas," is of the same order of pomposity as calling a close friend on the phone and identifying yourself by your full name such as "this is J. William Schlitz."

In practice there are many viewpoints held by managers and department heads who have no background that qualifies them to make such detailed decisions. Then it is the cliche line, "I don't know anything about art, but I know what I like," that applies. Viewpoints are especially diverse among stations whose managers have no specific background of qualifications for management. In many small-market stations, the manager holds his position because of a good record in programming or sales. Sometimes a manager is brought in from completely foreign fields and is without qualification to make detailed decisions in any department—announcing, copywriting, engineering, sales, or administration. One such manager, by virtue of a minority stock interest, took over management of a station in a city named Fayetteville. After two months' experience in the field of communication, he decided that the pronunciation of trained and competent announcers was too artificial. He decreed that the name of the city should be pronounced as the semi-literate and uncaring man-on-the-street pronounced it. Henceforth, on that station's air waves the name of the city sounded something like "Fedvul," a most incongruous sound from otherwise careful and precise professional announcers.

The general public looks to professionals for correctness. How many times have you seen advice in newspapers and magazines to "listen to radio and TV announcers for correct pronunciation." The same respect for professional knowledge extends, at least by projection, to writing for the announcers.

The thinking that small-town listeners should be presented a writing style that is on a level with their own lack of knowledge and literacy is consistent with the thinking of many small-town weekly newspaper publishers. Many of them excuse their sloppily edited papers on the grounds that, "people around here are uneducated and unsophisticated. They wouldn't understand professional writing and editing." The fact is that the rural weekly's circulation figure is almost exactly equal to the total of city dailies circulated in its market, an indication that most newspaper readers read both the local weekly and one of the city dailies. The same readers are also listeners to both local radio and network radio and television. Comparison is unavoidable. This would seem to be sufficient reason to adhere to the best editing practices in any medium. The designation "downtown," except in the case of a low-power station in a city of half a million or more, would appear to be an error. In small and medium markets, especially where your station handles advertising for suburban or out-of-town retailers, it is better practice to use the name of the town. Like this: "Go to Sadlers tonight and pick the one you want. Sadler Chevrolet, Third and Main, Columbia." Or if the downtown designation is desirable, write it: "Sadler Chevrolet, Third and Main, downtown Columbia." Further comments on editing practices will be found in Chapter 9.

Chapter 8

Power With Short Copy

Here are some guidelines for writing effective short copy:

1. Use sound whenever possible.

2. Use various production techniques and dialogue whenever possible to cram all the power and emotional appeal possible into the time.

3. Use an emotional sensitizer.

4. Follow the emotion with an unmistakably clear point.

5. Drive the point in with a sledge hammer if necessary.

6. Stick to **one** point; don't try to support it with allied ideas.

7. Follow the AIDA formula, just as in longer copy.

Shorter copy has become more prevalent for several reasons. Probably the most effective force in the trend toward more short radio copy has been the advertisers' experiences in television. This refers to national advertisers who tend to establish trends.

The tremendous costs of television have driven many advertisers to 20- and 30-second spots in order to get both reach and depth, in other words, more impressions on more people for the same budget.

As copywriters have felt the crunch of necessity, they have found ways to make short copy stronger. Short copy in television is doing a good job for advertisers and the demand for similar results is being felt in radio. Another reason is a general adherence to the NAB Code of Practice which requires a limit on the number of commercial minutes per hour. This is a purely business reason based on increasing station revenue while operating within the limits of the code.

Eighteen commercial minutes per hour is permitted by the code. This, of course, allows time for 18 one-minute spots or 32 half-minute spots, or some combination of the two. Since half-minute spots usually are priced at 60 percent of the one-minute rate, more revenue is produced by using shorter copy. By using this concept a station can schedule 20 to 25 spots per hour without exceeding the minutes-per-hour limit.

Traditionally, another reason has been the ignorance of local advertisers who simply buy the lowest rate on the card because it is the lowest. Research over the years has shown that 60-second spots are most effective in telling the client's story and in motivating listeners to act. Local advertisers generally are unaware of such useful information and are rarely educated fully by station personnel. A station salesman is likely to make the prospective advertiser a pitch for 60-second spots and then settle for whatever the prospect is willing to buy. If the prospect insists on buying a less effective schedule, the salesman is hardly in a position to refuse to sell it to him, or take his order. Thus have been created many dissatisfied advertisers.

One fact that has come from the television cost crunch is this: Short copy can be effective. Professional copywriters faced with the necessity of jamming effective power into 20 and 30 seconds have done it. On the station level it has been rare because the agency-type pressure that comes from having 16 layers of supervisors looking over the copywriter's shoulder has been absent.

POWERFUL SHORT COPY IS POSSIBLE ON THE STATION LEVEL

As a station copywriter you can produce powerful short copy. It is written according to the same AIDA formula you follow on longer copy. The difference is not just a condensation of the same material, but a concept of slamming the bull's-eye hard and fast. In the Frigidaire appliance copy for Morris Furniture Stores in Chapter 6, one point is made: If you can afford seven dollars a month you can afford an appliance at Morris Furniture. By the use of emotional dialogue, the point is made clearly and effectively.

Use Emotion

Emotion has been compared to the light-sensitive coating of photographic film. When the film is exposed to light, the image focused on the film is etched into the coating. When the human mind is coated with a layer of emotion, the idea focused on the mind will be etched in the coating, just as a photographic image becomes part of the film.

In writing short copy the following rule is even more important than in long copy:

First EMOTIONALIZE

Then RATIONALIZE

By laying on the emotional appeal first, you sensitize the prospect's mind to the image you wish to etch therein. You know from your own growing-up experiences that you remember things associated with anger, unusual happiness, or embarrassment much more vividly than routine happenings that you went through many times without unusual emotion.

In short copy you don't have time to spread it smoothly, sponge it off, and wipe it down neatly as you sometimes do in longer copy. Many times you must throw on the emotion with a shovel; lob in your rationalization like a hand grenade and run. Your time is up.

The Morris Furniture example in Chapter 6 does it all. Go back and check it again. First, it prepares the mind for receptivity with a fast blast of domestic emotion. Then it dumps a load of rationalization and runs offstage with the agreement that "we'll go look." That's all. The point is driven into the prospect like a harpoon—fast and hard. There's no time to develop an idea, to expand on supporting issues. Your job is to pick one point and drive it home.

The technique bears a definite similarity to the scenes in war pictures where the hero scampers across an open space to the wrecked farmhouse, leans momentarily around a corner and tosses a grenade through the window. Then he ducks behind the wall and stands quietly with a happy look of anticipation on his face. He has done his job. But the explosion is yet to come.

Argument or anger are not the only emotions that are effective. Use your imagination and reasoning power to find a sensitizing agent for your prospect's message. Almost any conversational exchange that shows love, yearning from some specific emotional satisfaction, enjoyment, appreciation, etc., is effective. Go back and check the example of feminine voices gloating over a desirable dress (it's in Chapter 3).

Make it a habit to check magazine advertising for emotional sensitizing ideas and make notes of good ideas you see on TV. The best agency copywriters are assigned to TV copy. You can learn from their work. Beware of local advertising in newspapers—even in larger cities. Chances are you can write far better copy based on a more solid foundation of effective appeals.

One off beat technique was used about 1966 to produce spectacular sales for an off brand oil company in the midwest. In 1969 Ultra Brite tooth paste took the idea. It depends on pure nonsense, but it is a happy type of nonsense that keeps repeating the point that great things happen to you when you use Ultra Brite.

Here is a flexible idea. It can be cut to 20 seconds or continued as long as may be desirable. It's done in short takes, each of which can stand alone as an emotional sensitizer:

1st WOMAN: **How was your trip?**

2nd WOMAN: **Wonderful. Met more good lookin' fellows than last trip.**

1st WOMAN: **Change ships?**

2nd WOMAN: **No. Changed to Wizzo hair spray. (giggly laughter)**

SOUND: **STINGER**

ANNCR: **The now generation discovers a secret weapon. Whizzo, the hair spray with sex appeal. It can change your whole life.**

1st WOMAN: **It sure is a lot more fun at the rent-a-car desk since I started using Whizzo hair spray. The fellows used to take cars out. Now they take me out. (giggly laughter)**

SOUND: **STINGER**

1st MAN: **The wildest thing happened to my wife since she started using Whizzo hair spray. This groovy, handsome man has fallen in love with her.**

2nd MAN: **Really? Who is he?**

1st MAN: **Me! (wild laughter)**

SOUND: **STINGER**

ANNCR: **Whizzo hair spray. The bright look, the now look, the kicky look; that's sex appeal. It's a fact. After Whizzo everything else is just hair spray.**

SOUND: **MUSIC FLOURISH.**

Notice the short sentences. Some of them violate the rule against writing in telegraphic style. But this is a type of speech that is normal in conversation. There are exceptions to all copywriting rules and this is one of them. Anything that sounds like normal conversation and gets your point across is useful.

This technique of nonsense copy could be used for almost any type of business at the local level. Consider what you might do with it for a tire recapper, a drug store, a service station, a bread bakery, a body shop, a flying school, an apartment complex. It is especially good for stores or products that have no really distinguishing characteristics, when you need to sell a favorable image because there is very little real difference to sell. The cigarette market is a classic illustration of a situation made for image building. Blindfold tests have proven that smokers in general cannot tell one brand from another by taste. A research firm executive said they're smoking an image, but what an image.

A Marlboro smoker is puffing on "great, sweeping, rugged, he-man territory." A Silva-Thin smoker is carrying a tall, thin package of "bright, tough-minded sophistication" in his pocket. And an Ultra Brite user is squeezing "sex appeal onto her tooth brush." What kind of image can you create for a local business? Dream up a good idea, put it on paper, and chances are you can sell it. This is a good technique to use for short copy. An entire campaign, using this type of copy, could be carried out with 30-second spots. The object is to create an image in the minds of your listeners. Since an image is not necessarily logical, you don't need reasons why, just copy that makes one point: wonderful things happen to you when you...

It would be a mistake, however, to go about creating images without regard to realities. Here are some points to consider.

Reality number 1: Your advertiser is local, therefore, visible.

Reality number 2: Many listeners may know almost as much about your advertiser as you do.

Reality number 3: It would be a mistake to try to create the image of a glamorous, elegant, jet-set watering place for a restaurant which features a 95-cent businessman's lunch served on Formica-topped tables with stainless steel tableware and paper napkins. It would be an error to try for an image of overwhelming friendliness and helpfulness for a serve-yourself discount store.

Reality number 4: Since your local advertisers are somewhat more tangible than Marlboro smoke, the image must have some realistic relationship to the business.

Reality number 5: A realistic relationship can be quite tenuous and still be quite effective. To a young fellow who owns his first T-Bird, or to a teenager driving his first $200 jalop, the suggestion that wonderful things happen to bright young men who have their cars serviced at Bob Smith's Westside Texaco can set up some interesting chains of thought. A suggestion that wonderful things happen to young men who learn to fly is even more thought provoking. The possibility that a girl who changes jobs may meet the man; that good things happen to you when you make a habit of driving into the Ajax drive-in every time you're out driving; or that the use of good recapped tires is a mark of automotive knowledgeability, is realistic. They do no violence to your prospects' existing knowledge or convictions.

Copy of the same construction as the Whizzo hair spray example can be used for serious testimonial copy. The only difference is that you would make serious points instead of nonsense points. Either type can be short, medium, or long.

There is, of course, the possibility of using a testimonial type of copy without having actual testators, but you must be careful not to offend the Federal Trade Commission's sensibilities by misleading your listeners. One effective way to use this is to have a series of three or four unprofessional voices make one statement each in a halting manner as though they were being interviewed and were thinking out the answer as they talk thoughtfully. For example:

1st GIRL: ...well ...uh ...I didn't much think I'd like it but I tried it and I've been using it ever since.

1st MAN: ...uh ...and then I tried it and my wife grabbed it and tried it, and we've sort of been using it ever since, you know.....

2nd GIRL: ...and I just sort of like the taste of it...

2nd MAN: ...so I ran out of my own brand one night and asked one of the fellows in the dorm to lend me his... and... well, I've been using it ever since.

This technique can be used to get across any point you may wish to make. It is simply dialogue copy done in actual conversational style. Instead of the practical exaggeration or overacting necessary for the usual commercial, this is done as though you had taped a very dull and low-key phone conversation and cut out a few inches at random for the commercial. The sound is a monotone, a legible, high-grade mumble. It's a sound that comes mostly from the throat rather than the diaphram. For that reason it is difficult for some experienced announcers to produce.

While this technique may appear to violate the principles followed by most successful advertising, it clobbers the target in strict accord with one well-known competitive principle. That's the old baseball adage, the manager's advice to his batters to "hit'em where they ain't." As Joseph Stone said in Jacksonville, "When everyone starts doing short operas, do burlesque."

Chapter 9

Power Through Mechanics

Most of the mechanics of writing copy are based on pure common sense. However, some, not immediately obvious, have been developed by good copywriters over many years. The following list includes many of the mechanical aspects that successful pros have learned.

1. Keep sentences short enough so that announcers can breathe easily.

2. Use words and phrases that are suitable to the personality of both the talent and the product.

3. Write smooth, easily readable sentences with as many words as necessary to make them sound natural.

4. Eliminate all unnecessary words.

5. Direct the copy to a single individual.

6. Furnish announcers absolutely clean copy whenever possible.

7. Use type that is most acceptable to announcers.

8. Set the typewriter for 10-word lines.

9. Make positive statements. Avoid negatives.

10. Write several pieces of copy for the same client at the same time.

11. Avoid the use of print media references.

KEEP SENTENCES SHORT

For any writer who also does air work it is unnecessary to even state this rule. A writer who has never sat at an open mike reading a sentence that appeared to have no end has missed an educational experience. The principle is simple. Give the announcer reasonsable opportunities to breathe normally. When it is necessary or desirable to write a longer sentence that could create a breathing problem, be sure it is punctuated properly. A comma or a semicolon can provide a breathing place, but a period is better.

The problem is common to all professionals in oral communication. In the mid -50s, June Carter, an irrepressible member of country music's Carter Family, filled the B side of a record with a song bewailing another song's lack of a "swallerin' place."

The use of short sentences is desirable for two reasons. First, they put punch and power into your copy. Second, a sound of enthusiasm is easier to maintain with short sentences. Here's an example of strong copy written with short sentences. Notice the power that comes from starting new sentences.

ANNCR: Your car needs a summer checkup for the little things as much as for the big things. Just as much. Your car doesn't have to start falling apart before Bob's Westside Texaco starts tightening the loose nuts and bolts. Ninety percent of preventive maintenance is related to the small problems—before they get to be big problems. Things like a worn fan belt, worn generator brushes, a loose wing nut on the air filter. Bob's Westside Texaco takes care of the little things, as well as the big things.

The first sentence and the following fragmentary sentence could have been combined but the emphasis gained in the 3-word sentence would have been lost, completely lost. Editing of unnecessary words contributes to short sentences. Look for unnecessary words in this copy. You won't find any. It's slim, trim, simple and understandable. As simple and understandable as "Look, look, see Jane read the book," but more effective.

Jack Webb is master of the short punchy sentence. Perhaps you recognize these:

Then it becomes my business. I carry a badge.

I just want the facts, Ma'am.

And then what happened?

Did you see him pull the trigger?

Maybe!

Short, every one of them, but everyone is jammed full of power.

Such extremely short sentences are inappropriate to some types of copy. Fashion copy, for instance. Longer, smoother sentences, flowing with a powerful stream of enthusiasm, painting a beautiful and glamorized picture, are effective in making your prospects react, believe, buy.

Read the preceding sentence aloud. See how the natural pauses give time for breathing without interrupting the flow of the sentence. That's because the sentence builds from one phrase to the next. It builds to a climax, the point of it all. You can breathe after the words sentences, enthusiasm, picture, if you wish. Most announcers probably would breathe only after enthusiasm and picture. But the opportunities are there. Better to have them and not need them than need them and die waiting for one.

Notice in the example that descriptive phrases are strung in series, building toward the climax, the peak of the mountain of logic. At the end of the sentence is the point of it all—a series of three words: "react, believe, buy." This technique multiplies the impact, socks the listener with the souped-up power of five ideas to drive home one point.

One seemingly insignificant but highly important point to observe in writing longer sentences is this: **Use correct punctuation.** Do not use an ellipse as a substitute for a comma. This is an ellipse: ... and it denotes a longer pause or hesitation than normal punctuation can. When used as a substitute for a comma, semicolon, or period, it is lazy copywriting, leaving the announcer to do the punctuating for you. The way to get good copy aired correctly is to punctuate it correctly. You do the punctuation. Leave nothing unnecessarily to the judgment of announcers. They may have the best of intentions, as well as some excellent ideas of their own, but less knowledge of your concept (and perhaps that of your client). A good announcer will read a period, comma, semicolon, and exclamation mark as effectively as if you had written out complete stage directions for him. Each mark has a different meaning and is interpreted differently for your listeners.

One point of confusion can be cleared up easily. The practical difference between a period and a semicolon is in the way you want the sentence interpreted. A semicolon is used properly between two main clauses, each of which **could** be used as a complete sentence or fragmentary sentence by inserting a period. For example:

ANNCR: Your car needs a summer checkup for the little things as much as for the big things; just as much.

In the original example of this same copy a period was used instead of the semicolon. Either punctuation is grammatically correct, but the use of a period gives the announcer instruction to put more punch into the second sentence than he would if a semicolon were used. A semicolon may be used without a conjunction (and, but, or so, etc.) between clauses. It is also properly used between phrases which are used in series.

USE WORDS AND PHRASES SUITABLE TO THE PERSONALITY AND THE PRODUCT

This is just good sense. When you write that the Cobra Ford "was raised in a tough neighborhood; Ford puts the money in the muzzle and gives you a car born to move," obviously you want the powerful voice of a man. This would be inappropriate for a woman. It is conceivable that copy appropriate for a woman's delivery could be written to convey the same image, but it would be vastly different.

Delicate words written in fanciful flight of fashion fantasy are just as obviously inappropriate when delivered by a man. There is a fine line here, but important. In regard to fashion, the word "lovely" is best left to feminine talent. Gorgeous, striking, and other such descriptive words are appropriate and paint a more accurate picture.

WRITE SMOOTH, EASILY READABLE SENTENCES

Radio copy is for listening, not reading. It should sound natural to your listeners. Not only are complex and unusual words distracting and confusing, so are complex or overly simplified sentences. Do not write in telegraphic form. That is appropriate to print media where the eye picks the key words quickly. When the listener hears the same information, it is more effective when it comes in the way he expects to hear such information: in complete sentences. Here is newspaper advertising copy taken from a typical furniture ad:

Bonus sale! Pay no money down. Only $29.23 per month. Look what you get as a bonus gift with the purchase of this 3-room group.

These are short sentences but not connected like good radio copy. When the newspaper reader sees the pictures, this billboard-like copy tells him something about what he's seeing. If the same copy is heard, instead of read, there is something missing. The sentences are incomplete. The picture is not all there. In the series of three short sentences not one is complete. They are what is known as fragmentary sentences. (One can be considered complete including an **understood** element, but we won't get into an English teacher-type discussion about that.)

The important **radio copy** ingredient missing is the grammatical reference. One of those fragments needs—for radio purposes— to be filled out with a reference to the subject matter. The subject is the 3-room group and the above way of handling it is satisfactory for print. The reader can always re-read to refresh his memory and to put two or more printed thoughts together in his mind. But the listener must have it all presented as clearly as possible because he can't look back. Something like this would adapt the copy for listening:

ANNCR: **You don't need a down payment at Winston-Franklin's exciting bonus sale. Look over the 15 styles of fine furniture and select what you need to fill any three rooms in your home. Then have them delivered. Pay nothing down. Use your fine furniture, hear the extravagant compliments of friends, neighbors and relatives for a full four weeks before you make the first low monthly payment of only $29.23. As a bonus for deciding THIS WEEK on the three rooms of furniture you want, you'll get free—with no additional cost whatever—a breath-taking 95-piece tableware set.**

ELIMINATE ALL UNNECESSARY WORDS

While it is desirable to use more words than typically found in telegraphic print copy, it is just as desirable to keep the words to a necessary minimum. This accomplishes two purposes:

A. Often, the elimination of surplus words is the only means of fitting an otherwise good piece of copy into the specified time limit.

B. The time saved by the elimination of useless words can be used for a constructive purpose by adding working words.

Books could be, and have been, written on the many aspects of copy editing. One of the best and most useful is **The**

Careful Writer, by Theodore M. Bernstein, published by Atheneum. Bernstein, an assistant managing editor of the New York Times, is responsible for what is known in that profession as the "style" of the publication's nonadvertising matter. And it is to the New York Times, along with the St. Louis Post-Dispatch and the Christian Science Monitor (and possibly one or two others), that the dictionary editors turn for information on changes in word usage.

It is said that dictionary editors count the way a particular word is used in every issue of those papers for one year when considering an alteration of their definition of it. Consequently, obtaining the opinion of the man who first decides on the appropriateness of those words is the equivalent of getting the word from the horse's mouth. Bernstein's goal is to have the written word say exactly what the writer intended to say—no more; no less. A goal, it can be seen, that is most appropriate for every radio copywriter. The book retails at $7.95 and is strongly recommended (in Number 2 priority) for the desk of every copywriter. First a good dictionary, then Bernstein's The Careful Writer. Any good bookstore has it or will get it for you.

Notes on the dust jacket say that the book is a modern guide to English usage, "concise, yet a thorough handbook, covering in more than 2,000 alphabetized entries the problems that give (or should give) a writer pause before he sets words to paper: questions of use, meaning, grammar, punctuation, precision, logical structure, and color.

"It is perhaps the liveliest and most entertaining reference work for writers of our time; delightful while it instructs, amusing even as it scolds and cajoles the reader into skillful, persuasive, and vivid writing," the notes observe.

One type of editing help that comes from the book is skill in shortening sentences by eliminating common words written automatically but not missed when deleted. One copywriter has written "the cost is small when measured in terms of decades." Bernstein would point out that the sentence loses nothing when "terms of" is deleted.

The Number 3 priority writing aid is a copy of Roget's (pronounced Ro Gay's) Thesaurus, a volume of synonyms, cross-indexed. Many times you can find the perfect word for the image you want to project in your copy. It is the opposite of a dictionary; you turn to it when you have the meaning but don't yet have the word. You know well enough that the other words you try won't do. They say too much or too little, or they are too flat or too showy, too kind or too cruel. But the just right word won't come, so you reach for your Thesaurus.

It's a relatively expensive book, but a paperback version at less than a dollar should be sufficient for a good copywriter. You have no use for the more obscure or esoteric words. One top-selling novelist says that a Thesaurus is a liability. If you can't find a suitable word in a good dictionary, you're getting too high-flown for your audience. That's one man's opinion. Other good writers tend to disagree to some extent. The author's advice is to use every advantage, every time-saver, and every quality-inducing help available to you. At the same time, use your best judgment in choosing the words that will direct your client's message to his prospects.

Other helpful books and reference material include one of the many lists of words frequently misused. It will give you such information as this: "Individual" is an adjective describing a person or thing, not a noun designating a person. Don't use individual when you mean person. There is one exception. Example: ...will be sold either to corporations or individuals. A librarian or book store manager can direct you to several books of this type. Frequent reference to a good collection of such information will do much to tighten your writing and make it say exactly what you want it to say—to project the exact image you wish to impress on your listeners.

DIRECT YOUR COPY TO ONE PERSON

Write all your copy as though it were intended for one listener alone. This is direct communication. You may think of your listeners as a mass. But a listener thinks of himself as one person. In most cases he is listening alone, so you really are addressing one person.

Have you noticed advertising along the roadside addressed to "tourists?" "Tourists Welcome." "Special Welcome to Tourists." "Tourists Information." Chances are none of those signs applied to you. You may have been on vacation. You may have been driving through. You may have needed some of those services. But you didn't think of yourself as a tourist. You were simply driving through on vacation. The copy is oriented to the advertiser's viewpoint, not yours.

You may drink and enjoy beer. But chances are you include yourself out when an announcer says, "here's a good word for all you beer drinkers." You do not consider yourself as part of a mass of "beer drinkers." You are an individual person with your own tastes and preferences.

The fact that you like a good beer now and then does nothing to lessen your individuality. Beer is simply an individual enjoyment for you. Other persons may enjoy beer, too, possibly the same brand as you. But who cares? Not you! A taste for good beer is not a link that joins you to a mass of strangers with one similar interest like membership in Woodsmen of the World, Kappa Sigma, or the International Concatenated Order of Hoo Hoo.

When the announcer says, "here's a good word for all you beer drinkers," he isn't talking to you. He's talking to a mass of strange beer drinkers you'd probably be just as happy not knowing. To grab your attention and interest he must talk directly to you. For example:

ANNCR: If you like a good beer..."

Aaah. That's more like it. Now he's talking to you.

By the same reasoning, neither are you "one of those." You've seen printed advertising and probably heard it on the air, too, "designed for those who care," "those who know fine furniture," "those who ..." ad infinitum, ad nauseum. You are not one of "those." You are you! And you respond more readily when identified and treated as you. So do your listeners.

The word "those" is a two-edged sword that can cut both ways, but there's a better way to get across your idea, however; consider this: The word "those" can generate some social climbing and allied motivations. A supper club advertising (somewhat pompously to be sure): "We cater to those who care" may, for that reason, attract customers who want to be known to care or who want to be seen rubbing elbows with those presumed to care.

Generally, the individual approach would be better here, too. "If you enjoy an evening out in a lush atmosphere, a restaurant where major decisions are made over a steak and a drink, etc...."

FURNISH ANNOUNCERS CLEAN COPY WHENEVER POSSIBLE

In many stations it is possible to provide clean copy much more often than it is done. Quite often it is necessary to yank a first draft out of your typewriter and rush it into the control room. But those occasions should be relatively rare. Some of them can be avoided by better planning. Others are unavoidable and must be lived with serenely.

Clean copy, whenever possible, is the very least an announcer has a right to expect from a copywriter. Clean copy with no obvious strikeovers, no XXXXXs, and no pencil corrections, insures that the announcer will view your copy with more respect. He's likely to take it at the value you put on it. If it's sloppy copy, then that's just what he will assume it is—sloppy copy. He can't get enthusiastic about it if you don't. If you take the time to finish a neat, fresh final draft, then he will view it with considerably more respect and enthusiasm, enthusiasm that will be evident in his delivery.

USE TYPE THAT IS MOST ACCEPTABLE TO YOUR ANNOUNCERS

Exhaustive tests over many years have demonstrated conclusively that the usual print combination of caps and lower case letters is the easiest to read. Yet many stations persist in using all capital letters for copy simply because it has been traditional, as broadcasting traditions go, and many announcers prefer it simply because they have seen copy in all caps since their first day on the air. It is not a matter for great concern, but if a change could be made to the more readable combination of caps and lower case, some improvement in the readability of your copy would be observed. Before making such a change it would be well to consult all announcers, explain the reason, and make sure you will not be creating hostility.

SET YOUR TYPEWRITER MARGINS FOR 10-WORD LINES

Using 10-word lines makes your copy easy to time. For 50 words you need five lines. For 100 words you need 10 lines and for 150 words you need 15 lines. As you may remember from high school typing class, the average word has five characters. Allowing for eight spaces between words, a 10-word line would measure 58 spaces on your typewriter scale. If the middle of the scale is 50, set your left margin at 21 and the right margin to give an average line ending on 79.

MAKE POSITIVE STATEMENTS—AVOID NEGATIVES

This is basic to advertising, selling, and all efforts in the field of marketing and human relations. Avoid communicating in a negative manner unless you have a particular purpose in using the negative. When you check into a motor hotel and the clerk says, "don't have but one left and it's upstairs," you begin to doubt the desirability of the room and perhaps wish you had driven on and tried another hostelry. You might even decide not to take the room. However, if the clerk had taken a positive attitude and said "I have a beautiful room for you, convenient to the dining room and overlooking the pool," you would have been perfectly satisfied.

An elderly small-town merchant in South Carolina tells the story of how he became convinced of the value of a positive attitude:

"We heated the store with a pot-bellied coal-burning stove then. One of my good customers, a farmer, came in, hurried on back to the stove where several of us were standing. I commented to him about the terrible weather, and the tragic effect the weather could have on farm crops. And I predicted that it was going to be a long, hard winter with hardships for many people in the county.

"After a few minutes of this kind of conversation the farmer started to leave without having bought anything. I jokingly asked if he'd forgotten what he came in for. He said 'no, I came in to buy an overcoat but you've convinced me that I better save my money'."

In its simplest application to radio copy, this means: "Remember, nine o'clock tomorrow morning." Not "Don't forget, nine o'clock tomorrow morning." Tell your prospect what you want him to do; not what you don't want him to do. Not only is it a more efficient use of words, it is more effective in motivating your prospect to move.

Guide your prospect's thoughts the way you want them to go, not the way you don't want them to go. You must use this principle in a subtle manner many times to get across—in a positive manner—information that actually is negative. Your furniture store client says, "These lousy tables were all scratched up in transit. We'll have to unload'em at half price."

You write: "Choose one of these fine, hand-rubbed walnut coffee tables in a style that harmonizes with your living room. Because of careless handling in transit you may find a tiny scratch on some of them. That's why the entire group of 50 tables is marked down to half price. Winston-Franklin's loss is your gain."

Another subtle use of the positive statement is necessary in communicating negative information of a different type. Suppose your client, a shock absorber manufacturer, wants to tell prospects that many lives have been lost because of worn-out shock absorbers that let the car sway dangerously. He has no documentation to indicate that this is the case. There is no useful evidence that worn-out shock absorbers can be blamed for any specific accident.

At the same time he does have a substantial body of evidence that points in that direction. However, he cannot in good conscience make the flat statement that "a large number of accidents" or "a substantial number of accidents" or "a good percentage of accidents" have been caused by worn-out shock absorbers. To tell the story that he wants to tell, which in its simplest version is that worn-out shock absorbers **do** cause many accidents and deaths, you must make a negative statement in a positive manner. The statement an agency copywriter used to solve that problem is this:

ANNCR:　　**(COLD) No one knows how many accidents and deaths have been caused by worn-out shock absorbers.**

That tells the story and lets the listener make his own estimate, which undoubtedly is higher than any evidence would indicate.

The above violates the principle that a cure sells better than a preventive; therefore, it is better to advertise the cure possibilities. The client was Monroe, and the jury is still out as this is written. If the same pitch is continued, you may conclude that the principle was violated successfully.

Here's a horrible example of negative newspaper copy for a Nashville furniture store. It is quoted here because it is typical work of an untrained copywriter. Similar mistakes are made in radio copy every day by writers who haven't taken the trouble to learn how to do their jobs. Under the headline "Mediterranean Accents" in three-quarter-inch letters, the lead copy block continues:

The charming little pieces that decorate the house. They give style and excitement to the rest of the furnishings. Without them things are just plain dull. For this week we are having an Early Summer

SALE

on accent pieces throughout the store.

This is followed by a feature box almost in the center of the half-page:

Please come in and get some decorating ideas from our staff of competent people. Even if you don't buy, you'll enjoy the fresh, new ideas that they can give you. They will enjoy working with you.

Several criticisms of this noncopy can be enlightening:

A. In the lead copy block, the emphasis is on decorating the house. The ad salesman (who probably wrote it) expected readers to do their own thinking and figure out for themselves how much more they would enjoy living among the "charming little pieces." Some readers probably did. Many others assuredly didn't.

B. The copy is related to dull household furnishings. That's what it says. So who cares? Keep turning and looking at other equally dull and "we" oriented copy.

C. There is no logical connection or transition between the "plain dull" idea and the following sentence announcing a sale.

D. The box copy starts by begging! "Please come in..." The way to entice a customer into the store is to hold out a carrot for him to want. Say in an appropriate way "You'll get this benefit when you come in because..."

E. The next sentence "even if you don't buy" is negative. The possibility of not buying should be ignored. The copywriter's subject should be the benefits the prospect can get by buying. He should ignore the possibility of not buying, completely—forever! His purpose in using the "don't buy" reference could have been served more effectively with two words "without obligation," or "no obligation."

F. The statement, "They will enjoy working with you" smacks of the social-worker attitude. It might be an earnest do-gooder trying to convince a not-so bright welfare client that he ought to go to night school and learn to read. The doer of good appears to be just a wee bit less bewildered by the complexities of life than her welfare clients, who are not sure they share her view of what constitutes "good."

It appears that the point was "you'll be welcome to browse and ask questions; our people won't consider you a nuisance even if you don't buy."

A positive approach like this would have been far better:

You'll appreciate the fresh, new ideas in home decor that our trained staff is eager to pass on without obligation.

WRITE SEVERAL PIECES OF COPY FOR THE SAME CLIENT AT THE SAME TIME

You'll find that each piece is better than the last. After you write four or five, chances are you'll discard the first one, which looked pretty good when you finished it. This is a time-saver in the long run. Each piece of copy you write on the same subject is successively easier, better, and faster.

You may find that it takes 15 minutes to write the first one. The second may be finished in 10, and the others in seven. If you write one piece of copy for the client today, another tomorrow, and another the following day, and still another on the fourth day, you'll have one hour invested in work that could have been done better in 39 minutes. See Mike Wyatt's three pieces of clever copy for Bob Drake Motors in Chapter 13.

AVOID THE MECHANICS OF WRITING FOR PRINT

Avoid this type of reference, which is perfectly all right for print, but ridiculous on the air:

A. The following:

B. The preceding...

C. The above...

BE CAREFUL AND REALISTIC WITH NUMBERS

A. Do not use telephone numbers unless the point of the copy is to grind the number into the minds of your prospects, in which case you will use it several times. Can you remember a telephone number when you hear it on the air?

B. For safety and accuracy in handling your client's prices, set a definite policy for writing prices, inform all air personnel of all details of that policy (you might post it in the control room or recording studio) and then stick to it. A good policy is to use the dollar sign and only the figures necessary, like this: $6, and this: $6.95.

In writing news or other material using large numbers, use no more than three digits for huge numbers. Use figures up to 9,000. For larger numbers use a combination of figures and words. This avoids throwing the announcer into a tizzy as he tries to figure out (without pausing) whether it's millions or billions or just a lot of thousands. For example:

10 thousand 391 dollars and 16 cents.

100 thousand 201 dollars and 3 cents.

10 million 110 thousand 571 dollars and 10 cents.

200 billion 191 million 673 thousand.

In general broadcast news writing practice, large figures are rounded off for easier understanding unless the exact figure is essential to the story.

Chapter 10

Power for Various Angles

A question, properly used, can yank your prospect right into the picture you're painting for his benefit. Consider the now familiar example of the beer lead: "If you like a good beer..." The same idea can be presented in a question and, depending on what follows, may be just as effective.

You can start your copy like this: "Do you like a good beer?" The idea is the same and pushes the "hot button" on the same people. Reaction is likely to be "Yes, why?"

The question gets your copy off to a fast start. There's no beating around the bush of logic to connect your lead with the next idea, which is intended to create interest. After the question, interest is already created. Your job then is to intensify your prospect's interest.

The question lead is a time saver. You're off and running, streaking out of the starting gate like Native Dancer at the Kentucky Derby. And if your question is properly chosen, the prospect is chasing along the track with you, inspired by the 3-pronged spur of a great lead. Those three prongs are:

1. Appeal to self-interest

2. With the right word, phrase, or sound, and

3. Curiosity

In the example, "Do you like a good beer?" the appeal to self-interest is fast and direct. It grabs the attention of every prospect who hears it, but bounces harmlessly off the ears of nonprospects. It gets the attention of prospects because it is the right phrase, "...good beer?" And it arouses the prospect's curiosity by making him wonder why the question is asked. He may continue listening to learn why.

A successful small-space newspaper campaign created by the author used a 3-word question to find prospects who were like a handful of needles in seven gigantic haystacks. The advertiser was the owner of a 40-unit apartment complex near

Ft. Rucker, Ala. Seventeen apartments were occupied at the beginning of the campaign and the figure had been getting smaller for each of the preceding nine months. Within eight weeks a waiting list has been created.

The copy consisted of about 50 words of description, with an urge to call or write for reservations. The lead was "Going to Rucker?" The 2-column by 2-inch ads were scheduled on alternate weeks in the small Army newspapers of seven posts which furnished officers for Ft. Rucker's training courses.

Of perhaps 15,000 to 30,000 readers on each post, fewer than 20 officers were prospects. The campaign was successful because the three words were designed to capture the interest of those prospects. The question, "Going to Rucker?" leaped out and pushed the hottest buttons in the breast of each officer who knew that he would, indeed, be going to Rucker in the next few weeks. This was a direct and unmistakable attention grabber for him. It appealed to his self-interest. It used the right word and the right phrase. It aroused his curiosity and it produced results.

It is desirable to use such truncated (chopped off) questions with care. Too often they lead only into a dull, worn-out phrase that kills interest. The technique has been over-worked and requires careful thinking to avoid falling into the cliche trap.

A cliche (pronounced clee-shay with the accent on the second syllable) is a worn-out and excessively dull phrase or manner of speaking. The first time it was used it was brilliant and colorful. It was so impressive and memorable that other people began to use it frequently. It spread around the English-speaking world. Now it is no longer brilliant, nor colorful, just dull. There is nothing brilliant nor interesting about copying the work of better writers.

Good writers avoid cliches as earnestly as they avoid grammatical errors. The reason is purely practical. It has nothing whatever to do with whims of English teachers. Cliches, precisely because they are old, worn out, and dull, have lost their impact.

Lawyers get by with impossibly dull writing because their clients are highly motivated to read the wills, contracts, and other instruments. We who must sweat to hold the listener's attention from one line to the next must use all the influence available to us. Consequently, it is better to find a new way, or at least avoid the deepest ruts, to communicate an idea to him. A new word, a new expression, a new attitude, may be the straw that breaks his resistance, when the same old worn-out words would have bounced off the armor of his inertia like hailstones from the pavement. (Not like water off a duck's back, please).

It is lazy writing to use cliches, an unthinking use of the fruits of another writer's efforts. A little more effort is required to find new ways of expressing an old idea. But the extra effort is what separates the pro from the amateur in any endeavor from golfing to writing. Free-lance writers for popular magazines must find new ways, or their material won't sell. Editors, who buy in an open market, simply won't buy cliches. Their constant cry is, "I need a fresh, new approach." So does the radio copywriter.

Somewhere along the road of your broadcasting career you have passed—or you will—the fork that separates the pros from the dabblers, or as Lou Nelson characterized them, those who are just passing through. One fork is taken by the pros who are constantly looking for a fresh, bright, dramatic way to put an old idea into words. Words that fire the prospect's imagination and push him into an inspiring new vision of success, happiness, or enjoyment.

Questions can be formulated for a lead on almost any type of copy. Here are several timely examples:

FASHION: Did you know that chartreuse is THE fashion color this year?

PRICE: Do you want the freshest spring style in town at $4.66 off?

UTILITY: Do you want a kitchen range that does your thinking for you?

INSTITUTIONAL: Did you know that Metropolitan Personality fashions featured at Winston-Franklin will put you at the head of the fashion parade?

PERFORMANCE: Who offers you a better performance, better track record, and more enjoyable driving than Cobra Ford? (Nobody, that's who!)

BARGAIN: 1st VOICE: Where can I buy eggs for 59 cents a dozen?

PUT POWER INTO YOUR COPY WITH A STATEMENT

You can use a statement—a simple declarative sentence—to pull your prospect into the picture you're painting for him. However, the process of moving a prospect into the area of interest with a statement requires more careful thought than the question technique. In asking a question, your best approach usually is to involve the listener directly and immediately by saying "Do you? or "Did you know?" But a statement can accomplish the same task when all three elements of a good lead are used. Notice how, in the following example, an appeal is made to self-interest with the right phrase, resulting in an arousal of the curiosity:

ANNCR   You'll go to the head of the fashion class when you choose chartreuse

The phrase, "You'll go to the head of the fashion class," appeals directly to self-interest with words that pull your prospect into the picture, she begins to wonder why?

You can go right down the list of question leads and transform each into a statement lead like this:

PRICE: You can have the freshest spring style in town at $4.66 off the regular price!

UTILITY: It's here now! A kitchen range that does your thinking for you

INSTITU-   Winston-Franklin's METROPOLITAN Personality
TIONAL: collection of fine fashions will put you out front in the fashion parade

PERFORM-   You get better performance, better track record, and
ANCE: more enjoyable driving with a Cobra Ford.

BARGAIN: Today and tomorrow you can get eggs at only 59 cents a dozen at Big Star supermarkets.

Different statements saying essentially the same things without involving the prospect would be far less effective. Imagine yourself face-to-face with a prospect in a store saying as so many full page newspaper ads do:

Winston-Franklin does it again! Here's the wonderful
Metropolitan Personality collection of fine fashions.

Does it make sense to spend the advertiser's money to congratulate the advertiser? From the standpoint of a store buyer it does. The buyer isn't the advertiser; she isn't spending her own money. She merely wants the advertising to enhance her own reputation. Her goal is to promote her own career with the same advertising that sells fashion.

Few department store managers are sufficiently astute in the field of advertising to understand what happens here. By the use of such tactics the buyer may promote herself a raise in her present job, be promoted to a better job, or catapult herself into a higher paying job with a competitor—at the expense of her employer's advertising budget, at the expense of less-than-possible sales volume. She may not see her goal in exactly that light, but she does see the results of her efforts as they relate to her and to the store rather than as they relate to the customers.

There is, of course, some foundation in folklore for self-congratulatory advertising. It is well known that, "If you don't toot your own horn no one else will." But like most proverbs and old sayings, it is only a half-truth and is vastly inappropriate as a foundation for successful advertising. In writing copy, as in face-to-face conversation, it is desirable to make every sentence point out benefits the prospect will get from the merchandise. You're making a strong effort in that direction when you use the word "you" in your statement.

PUT POWER INTO YOUR COPY WITH A COMMAND

By expressing your idea as a command you can inject another form of psychological power. A command snaps with authority, with superior knowledge, and with a strong urge. You can go down the list once more and formulate commands based on the same ideas:

FASHION:	LEAD the fashion parade in a dress of chartreuse, the season's striking, fashion-right color.
PRICE:	CHOOSE a fresh, figure-flattering spring style from Belk's and save $4.66.
UTILITY:	LET the brilliant new Ajax kitchen range from Winston-Franklin do your thinking.
INSTITU-TIONAL:	LEAD the fashion parade with styles from the Metropolitan Personality collection at Winston-Franklin.
PERFORM-ANCE:	GET better performance, a better track record, and more enjoyable driving with Cobra Ford.
BARGAIN:	GET your week's supply of eggs at only 59 cents a dozen, today at Big Star.

It is apparent that all ideas are not equally adaptable to all three techniques of sentence construction. The kitchen range example would appear to be more effective in the question form and weakest in the command form. Similarly, the performance lead appears to be stronger as a question, but the statement is also good. The idea used in the fashion lead dies when converted to a command, and also loses some of its power in the statement form. The institutional idea, weak and ineffective when expressed as a question or statement, is at its best as a command. These random examples, then, give a clear indication that it is desirable to make a careful choice of the form to give the most effective expression to your ideas.

The above examples all deal with leads, but the same type of sentence construction can be used in the body of your copy, depending on the idea you want to express and the way you want to treat it. A question can be used in the body of your copy like this: "Sooner or later you'll have one like it. Why not now? Select the..."

A command can be used effectively like this in the body of your copy: "See the brilliant new Metro collection at Winston-Franklin today. Picture yourself walking through life, the Metropolitan Personality blending delightfully with your own." Or it can be used as it was in the example of utility copy: "Quick, dash down to Winston-Franklin and see what they have done for you." Near the end of the same copy: "If it's a house dress you need, wake up!"

THE POWER OF THE MIDDLE MAJORITY

Mrs. Middle Majority is—or should be—the target of almost all your copy. She and her family comprise about 65 percent of the population of any typical town or city. She is seen by social researchers as controlling 80 percent of family spending. Researchers have found that her social status as a member of the middle majority of 65 percent tends to parallel her financial status. But not necessarily: Fig. 10-1 shows the size of the middle majority compared to the other population classes.

One writer on the subject determined that the tossed salad is a more reliable indicator of social status than is personal income. Persons or families can progress from one social level to the one immediately above, but are unlikely to move further upward regardless of financial status.

A person who was born into the lower middle class, which consists mostly of white collar workers and some skilled workers, can, by sustained and strenuous effort, progress into the ranks of the upper middle class. There he hob nobs with executives, owners of larger businesses, and professionals. The next step up the ladder is the lower upper class, which is inhabited by the newly rich. These men, who are truly wealthy, made it themselves, as distinguished from the upper upper class who inherited it.

The family which starts in the lower middle and climbs into the upper middle finds that, regardless of financial status, it faces a brick wall. It is as difficult to find acceptance beyond that wall as it is for an East Berliner to escape the Communists' barrier.

The above classifications were established for us in 1948 upon the publication of Lloyd Warner's book **Social Class in America.** He delineated six classifications:

1. **Upper upper:** Families with inherited wealth, the aristocrats

2. **Lower upper:** Newly rich

3. **Upper middle:** Larger business owners, professionals, executives

4. **Lower middle:** Mostly white collar workers, some skilled workers, and tradesmen

5. **Upper lower:** For the most part skilled and semi-skilled laborers

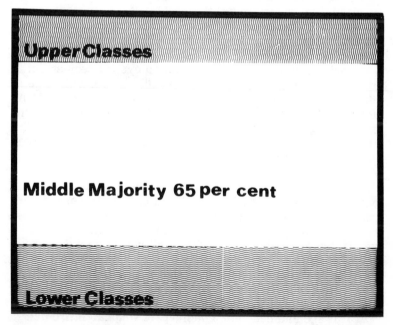

Upper Classes

Middle Majority 65 per cent

Lower Classes

Fig. 10-1. Graphic illustration of the American social strata.

6. **Lower lower**: Unskilled laborers and unassimilated foreigners

Other sociologists have reduced the classifications to five by combining the second and third groups into one. But this has no effect upon our consideration of the middle majority.

The upper classes, whether considered as two or three groups, constitute about 15 percent of the population. The lower lower group contains about 20 percent. That leaves about 65 percent of the population in the middle majority—upper lower and lower middle.

The middle majority is a tremendous concentration of purchasing power that makes advertising profitable. Research has uncovered several strong characteristics of Mrs. Middle Majority. A knowledge of them will help you create copy that relates merchandise to her needs and wants. You can see the influence of such knowledge in national advertising every day. Here are some of the characteristics that will help you find Mrs. M's reaction button:

1. Her life centers about her kitchen, which may be the nicest and most expensive room in her home. She tends to do most of her entertaining there. She is likely to have a pretentious, ornate dinette suite rather than a pretentious cherry, pecan, or mahogany dining room suite that Mrs. Upper Middle prefers.

Being kitchen oriented, she has an eye for recipes but is unlikely to try one calling for unfamiliar ingredients. She is likely to be a passable seamstress and sew for her children; and she is overwhelmingly enthusiastic about new or improved work-saving gadgets for her home—especially for the kitchen. Her kitchen is likely to have more and costlier gadgets than that of Mrs. Upper Middle.

2. She is quite unsophisticated about life that goes on outside her home. She is almost completely concerned with people and things. Ideas as principles and possibilities confuse her. She has limited imagination, and is inclined to wear a vague, tentative little smile when walking through a crowded room or store.

The realities of economics, the money market, politics, and propaganda are beyond her serious attention. She tends to believe the line of the last spokesman she saw and heard on TV. It is she and her male counterpart who catch fire over a politician's image without regard to substance. It is this majority that readily believes that an 8½ percent prime interest rate is the result of evil machinations on the part of bankers who arbitrarily decide to increase their profits. The effect of demand on supply is a strange and complex concept to her. She believes that "the company has plenty of money. They could raise wages if they wanted to." She is unable to understand that a man who employs a thousand people is contributing any more to the good of the community than is her husband who drives a fork lift.

3. Her emotional life is quite narrow, her moral code strong, and she is oppressed by a sense of guilt whenever she deviates from it. She is likely to work harder than other women, deriving more satisfaction from less meaningful work. She feels a personal responsibility for all housework and is gouged by guilt when such work is eliminated or simplified by technological progress. Manufacturers of ready-mixed cakes found that sales increased when they made the mixes harder to use and it became necessary for Mrs. M. to add a cup of milk or a couple of eggs. Their research revealed that she felt she was not doing right by her family when she merely ran a little tap water into the bowl before mixing and baking. She is likely to produce a sumptuous Sunday dinner because it is the thing to do, even when her family would prefer a quick snack.

4. Her tastes in entertainment are rather simple and uncomplex. This is revealed daily in soap operas which deal in basic human emotions: love, hate, and fear. Abstract questions such as "does the end justify the means?" leave her unmoved. Her taste in music crystallized on the day she was married. Her favorite songs are those popular in her premarriage days of romance. The Readers Digest has convinced her that all people are basically good; Walt Disney Productions may have convinced her that Mary Poppins is the best of all. She never heard of George Bernard Shaw's Pygmalion, but she stood in long lines to see it—as My Fair Lady, transformed into a sort of psuedo-sophisticated Mary Poppins.

Her 15-year-old child reads nothing in the newspaper except the comics, listens to nothing except rock and sports on radio, and leaves the room when the TV news begins. Yet she fumes about the reporting of innocuous details of sex crimes and gory murders, saying, "I don't want my children reading that kind of stuff."

5. Her reaction to free-wheeling ideas, uncontrolled impulses and emotional life is likely to be anxiety. A strong

theme of sexuality in advertising (such as some themes used in TV advertising for men's toiletries in the late sixties) is likely to provoke disgust. Her narrow little world is hemmed in by clock punching, children's activities, and a sorely limited budget. She is uncomfortable when her little boat is rocked and she sees unfamiliar waves rolling in from a world she has made no effort to understand.

6. She wants a positive black or white answer to any question involving her personal or family life. In her view, an action or a concept must be either black or white, right or wrong. She sees no reason for a gray area to exist.

Chapter 11

Putting Your "Hypnotic" Powers to Work

Madison Avenue has made a serious study of the techniques of hypnotism and ways they can be applied to advertising. Some effective ideas have come from such study. The results are quite evident in national advertising every day. Similar study and adaptation of the techniques of hypnotism can bring startling improvement to station-written copy.

To the uninformed (and that includes almost everybody) hypnotism appears to be a mysterious manifestation of dark or occult powers, powers used to control the actions of fellow humans with some kind of magical power of the mind. That is not the case at all. Hypnotism is simple, easily learned, and can be performed by any self-confident 15-year-old who will spend a few minutes learning how. The technique of hypnotism can be learned in less than half an hour. This is not to say that longer study is not necessary for mastery.

A word of serious warning, however, is in order. Although hypnotism is simple and easily learned, it is a powerful and potentially dangerous art. You could take the knowledge you are going to acquire here in the next three minutes and perhaps use it to hypnotize a friend or associate.

Don't!

A belief is becoming more and more prevalent that it should be practiced only by experienced psychologists or physicians. Since the practice of hypnotism is not controlled by law, experiments may be conducted by anyone who wishes. Some spectacular law suits have resulted from such activities on the part of inexperienced or irresponsible stage performers and amateurs.

Hypnotism is defined by most authorities as being a state of "heightened suggestability." That is the aspect of interest to you as a professional copywriter: heightened suggestability.

Except for some stage performers who have an exceptionally well-developed ability, it is generally true that a hypnotist cannot hypnotize an unwilling subject. There is a parallel principle of advertising you'll find explained in Chapter 12: Advertising won't sell merchandise that nobody wants.

The hypnotist begins the process of making his subject believe by explaining that he can put the subject into a trance only if he really wants to be hypnotized. This is not only the first step in the hypnotic process, it is, with rare exceptions, absolutely true. This is the beginning of the gentle but insistent and continuing suggestions that the subject will "go to sleep." Thus, the suggestion that the subject wants to be hypnotized is unobtrusively planted in his mind. Then, with the subject convinced that he is no longer a skeptic but one who now understands how the simple process of hypnotism works, the hypnotist begins the obvious suggestions.

Preferably the subject is put into a comfortable position, lying on a couch, or seated in a reclining chair where all muscles can be relaxed. The continuing suggestions begin. There is no standard or prescribed way to do it. But there is one principle that determines the success of the hypnotic effort: repeated suggestions. The same suggestion is made over and over.

It is well-known in office folklore that if the first few people you see in the morning tell you you're looking pale and unwell, you will indeed begin to feel weak and to detect symptoms of illness. It is the same power of suggestion, used more systematically, that puts the hypnotic subject into a trance. The hypnotist suggests over and over in a gentle, undisturbing manner, that "you're getting sleepy, your eyelids are getting heavier and heavier, you're getting sleepy, you're very sleepy, you can hardly hold your eyes open, you're getting sleepy..."

The hypnotist has techniques for determining the depth of the trance and deepening it if he wishes. It is a general belief of laymen that the subject is now "in the power" of the hypnotist. This is true only in the most limited sense. And that limit is one of the significant parallels between hypnotic techniques and advertising. You will find further elaboration on that point in Chapter 12.

As an advertising pro knows that prospects cannot be moved to buy something they do not want (a hand-operated windshield wiper, for instance), a practitioner of hypnotism knows that a hypnotized person cannot be forced to violate his own moral code. A stage hypnotist may bring out the ham in a hapless subject by successfully directing him to bark like a dog, or crawl around the stage on his hands and knees. But if the hypnotist directed the subject to commit murder, rob a bank, pick a pocket, or engage in sexual or other personal activities contrary to his normal way of life, the trance would be ended. The subject cannot be forced into such behavior and he cannot be forced to remain in the trance after such suggestions have been made. Usually, in such cases, the subject immediately comes out of the trance. Unless, during the trance, he was directed to forget—or told that he would not remember anything that transpired during the trance—he is likely to come out of it in a disturbed and unhappy state.

There is a message here for practitioners of the art of radio advertising who depend upon repeated suggestion to influence the behavior of prospects. The massive repetition of suggestions embodied in a sales message will influence the actions of a large number of people, just as continued and insistent repetition of the hypnotist influences the behavior of the hypnotic subject.

The parallel principle is this: Before **actions** are influenced, the hypnotic subject and the advertiser's prospect must be made to believe. The effort required of a hypnotist to put a new subject into a trance typically ranges from 5 to 15 minutes. Fifteen minutes consecutively, obviously, is more effective than three 5-minute sessions at the rate of one a day. For a subject who needs 15 minutes of suggestion, the shortened sessions over a 3-day period would produce no results at all.

In the 1930s when many major markets had two or three radio stations and medium markets had one or none, and there was no TV, each station maintained a massive audience. The number of sales messages to which the average American was exposed was quite small. Today it is estimated that the average person is exposed to more than 1,500 sales messages in various forms every day.

The market is fragmented, in contrast to the days when one 60-second spot on KWKH, Shreveport, was enough to move an entire day's production of one peach orchard. Well over half the radios turned on at any given moment in a radius of 100 miles were tuned to that station.

Today, one 60-second spot is a lost ball in the high weeds of fragmented audiences exposed to double, triple, and quadruple spotting all day long. To cut through the haze of commercials competing in a thousand different ways for the attention, belief, and memory of listeners, the hypnotic technique of continuing repetition has proved effective.

In earlier days of radio, one spot a day was an adequate schedule for some businesses. In the mid 40s an advertiser who scheduled five a day was living dangerously. Then research proved that a schedule of 10 spots a day was even more effective, per dollar cost, than five. It was only one easy step, then, for many hard-charging station executives and retail advertisers alike to find that 20 spots a day produced an even more favorable cost-effectiveness ratio.

The reason for the increased effectiveness is not that 20 spots a day reach more people than 10, although that is true, it is because effectiveness increases in a somewhat mathematical progression related to the number of repetitions. Stated another way, when repetition is increased, results increase faster than advertising costs.

Although there is a shortage of research in this area, it has been the author's experience that doubling the number of spots used by car dealers and promotion department stores from 10 to 20 a day consistently resulted in more than doubling the client's business for the day. The day's business was compared to previous days when only 10 spots were used. Presumably, such increases can be projected to other types of advertisers.

To translate these findings into effective practice, here are practical suggestions based on the author's own experience in markets ranging from 10,000 to 500,000.

If the client has a budget for 20 spots for a weekend sale, schedule them all on Friday. Or 10 Friday morning and 10 Saturday morning—no thinner.

If he has five spots for a weekend sale, schedule them in a 2-hour period on Saturday morning. It is easier to generate business when business is already good than to create good business on a slack day. This is why Coca-Cola budgets more advertising for the three summer months than for any other three months in the year.

If the client has a budget of three spots to promote a weekend sale, the sales rep should refuse to take it. You can't afford to have dissatisfied customers; that's what the client would be after your station invited him to go bear hunting with a pea shooter.

For a real door-busting, knock down, snatch and grab department store sale, schedule 20 spots a day every day of the sale, Monday through Saturday. This may require an educational effort because few small and medium market retailers are accustomed to thinking of spot schedules of that size. But it is worth while for station personnel to educate them to the fact that 20 spots in one day will produce more results than 10 spots each on two days.

In a market where spots average $3, a substantial retailer wouldn't consider a $30 newspaper ad. That amount of space wouldn't get enough results to pay for itself. But the same retailer is inclined to view $30 as absolutely tops for a day on radio. This is the fault of radio management as much as it is the store manager's ignorance, and it can be corrected with a little effort.

Daniel Starch & Staff, who for years has occupied something of the same position in the newspaper field that Hooper, Neilsen, Pulse and the American Research Bureau occupy in broadcasting, has demonstrated that increasing the size of a newspaper ad by 107 percent increased its readership by only 24 percent. He did not report sales results.

The divergence is a point of interest to both broadcasters and advertisers. Newspaper advertising depends upon visual impact and is governed by the law of diminishing returns. Larger space, after about 100 column-inches, does not attract the same number of readers per dollar as the first 100 inches.

Radio advertising depends upon the impact of repetition, the same principle that makes hypnotic subjects **believe**. This is essentially the same repetitive technique that can convince someone that he is becoming so sleepy he must close his eyes and sleep; the same repetitive technique that can convince him that the lighted end of a cigarette pressed against the palm of his hand is an ice cube.

The power of repeated suggestions convinces women in childbirth that they feel no pain whatever. It convinces dental patients that they feel no pain when a tooth is pulled without the use of an anesthetic. It convinces compulsive eaters that they are not, after all, hungry now. And it convinces smokers that they don't really want a cigarette now.

The hypnotic power of suggestion has been used to relieve severe pain of a chronic nature. A lawyer in Oklahoma, suffering from a bone disease which caused almost constant and excruciating pain in his leg, was taught to eliminate the pain by self-hypnotism. How he was taught is unimportant here. The point of interest is that a hypnotist made repeated suggestions that he could hypnotize himself, thereby eliminating the pain. The lawyer, in the deepest recesses of his mind, believed those suggestions. And **believing**, he did it.

He believed he could do it. **Believing**, he **knew** he could do it for the same reason that he knew he could command his arm to move, his elbow to bend, and his fingers to curve with the exact amount of pressure necessary to pick up a pencil from his desk. He knew both facts because both had been etched on his brain. They were etched there by different processes, but nevertheless they were there. One was as effective as the other because both constituted **unconscious** knowledge. You can find more complete and detailed explanations in any of several books on hypnotism. Most public libraries have several.

Hypnotic techniques are used professionally in many ways, short of putting the subject into a hypnotic trance, of course. An opthamologist (MD eye specialist) in South Carolina is a serious student of hypnotism. He described for the author the woes of one particular patient and how he ended them with one brief suggestion.

The patient was a 19-year-old college boy who had just begun to wear his first pair of contact lenses. As in many cases, the presence of the foreign objects against his eyeballs and under his eyelids caused discomfort. The doctor told him, truthfully, that discomfort was quite common at first but that it tended to diminish in a few days and eventually disappear. The boy's discomfort persisted. Over a period of two weeks he called the doctor several times to discuss his problem. Finally, he returned to the doctor's office and said he was almost positive that he had gotten the two lenses switched and was wearing the left lens in his right eye and vice versa.

The doctor, upon determining that the lenses had **not** been switched, merely put them on a handling tray and returned them to the boy. Pointing to each lens in turn, he said, "This is the left lens. This is the right. They'll be all right now." Greatly relieved, the boy inserted the lenses and a year later had reported no further discomfort. He believed because he had confidence in the doctor. And **believing**, he was as effectively hypnotized in that **one respect** as if he had been in a trance.

The same opthmalogist warned against amateur or frivolous use of hypnotism. "The law of compensation," he said, "can produce results ranging from merely annoying to permanently tragic." The doctor noted: "I could take a real introvert, quiet, shy, and retiring, and by hypnotism make him into a loud, extroverted back slapper. He could go on like that for a month or maybe a lot longer, possibly quitting his job in the post office to take a job selling used cars. And then one day he might grab an axe and split somebody's head open."

There is a school of thought which runs counter to that theory. Many capable practitioners and students of hypnotism state vehemently that the medical profession is merely manifesting selfishness in trying to keep hypnotism to itself.

Whatever that situation may be, it is especially well for anyone in the business of broadcasting to understand that hypnotic techniques, sufficiently effective to put listeners into a trance, must not be used on the air. There are not enough judges in the world to hear all the charges of invasion of privacy that would.arise from such a caper!

Not only has the principle of frequent repetition come to radio advertising from the study of hypnotism, but copywriters have learned to use repetition unobtrusively within spot copy. It has long been recognized by good copywriters that it is desirable to present the main idea three times in copy (provided there's enough time). And in broadcast copy it is desirable to present the name (not necessarily the full or official name) of the product or advertiser at least three times in each spot. Beyond that, however, is the desirability of repeating motivating words consecutively. This practice came directly from Madison Avenue's study of hypnotism. The face of broadcast copy has been changed by this principle. You can hear it every day in national advertising.

Assume that a key motivating idea is good taste. You can repeat it exactly as a hypnotist would do. Like this:

> **The Rich's label means the very essence of good taste. Good taste is the intangible quality that people suddenly sense when you walk into the room. You enjoy life more when you walk in fashions that radiate the elusive quality of good taste. Good taste is part of a better you.**

When your advertiser wants to impress an idea or an image on your listeners, this is one of the very best ways to do it. You can use the technique in either straight pitch or production copy. In production it is most effective when a second voice makes the second mention. Like this:

WOMAN: **The very first thing I look for in fashion is good taste.**

MAN: **Good taste is the very essence of Rich's fashions.**

It is important to repeat the word or phrase consecutively, just as it is important for the hypnotist to continue his suggestions uninterrupted for 15 minutes, rather than use three 5-minute sessions. Other words written between the repeated words, while perhaps desirable from the viewpoint of an English teacher who is not concerned with increasing sales, merely dilute the effectiveness of your repetition.

Other ways to accomplish the desired repetition can be found, too. In a fanciful or comic production spot, for instance, the spot or an episode within the spot could fade out on repetition. Like this:

> (Hollow, dream-like quality of sound) ...surrounded by good taste, good taste, good taste, good taste, good taste...(AND OUT)

Lou Nelson achieved massive repetition (as well as good taste) for a Morristown, N. J. restaurant like this:

SOUND: **LIGHT NEUTRAL MUSIC UP AND UNDER**

GIRL: If you were going to take a client to lunch, where would you take him?

LOU: I'd take him to the Wedgewood Inn in Morristown.

GIRL: If you were planning a wedding reception, where would you have it?

LOU: I'd have it at the Wedgewood Inn at Morristown.

GIRL: If you were going to honor loved ones with an anniversary, where would you celebrate it?

LOU: At the Wedgewood Inn in Morristown.

GIRL: There's an important business meeting coming up and you've been designated to find the proper atmosphere. What would be your choice?

LOU: The Wedgewood Inn in Morristown.

GIRL: If you were to take a beautiful girl out for dinner, where would you take her?

LOU: The Wedgewood Inn, in Morristown.

GIRL Do you think I'm beautiful?

LOU: Would you like to have dinner with me at the Wedgewood Inn in Morristown?

GIRL. I'd love it.

LOU: Saturday night?

GIRL Eight o'clock?

LOU Fine.

GIRL	I know the **Wedgewood Inn** is in **Morristown. But do you know where?**
LOU	**217 South Street.**
GIRL	**You don't say very much. But I like the way you wink. You know what? I'm looking forward to Saturday night at the Wedgewood Inn.**
LOU	**Me too.**
SOUND	**MUSIC UP AND OUT.**

There are many other possibilities; each depends on your need for the technique, your client, the nature of your copy, and your own imagination. Listen for examples on network radio and TV and on national spots. This is a sophisticated technique that has evolved directly from high-level thinking, research, and tests of skilled and respected practitioners of the art of advertising. You will not use it effectively in first draft copy. This is powerful medicine. Like much other medicine, it should be shaken well before it is taken.

Shake up your thinking. Try various combinations of repetition. Then decide which is best for your immediate purpose. Your writing must be smooth and logical, not contrived mechanically merely to accommodate repetition. It is neither easy nor fast, and it needs careful planning and thoughtful polishing.

Chapter 12

Powerful Copy Basics

As a result of the political climate in this country since 1932, when politicians and professors discovered (as did Ceasar) that the people will vote themselves corn from the public crib regardless of the long-range consequences, our colleges are graduating more and more students of divinity, law, social science, political science, education, and the liberal arts who condemn advertising as socially and economically undesirable. For the most part these people have unthinkingly accepted such erroneous principles on the authority of misguided faculty members who acquired them without question from their teachers.

The idea was promulgated seriously in this country in the 1920s by a very small but widespread group of social malcontents involved in the Communist movement and the IWW, a Soviet-oriented labor movement, soon discredited. Many of the youngsters who come out of college mouthing such nonlearning as "fifteen brands of toothpaste is wasteful," are unthinking and unknowing tools of shrewder men. The idea of eliminating advertising is based on the ultimate premise of government control of the means of production (farms, factories, mines, etc.) which is the foundation of political socialism, the utopian idea that has invariably led to the elimination of advertising and all other freedoms.

When a dictator, whether an individual person or a committee, decrees that there shall be only one brand of toothpaste, one type of automobile, one model of typewriter, one design of underwear, or one aroma of perfume, then, of course, advertising is unnecessary. What is necessary is to stand in line to buy the same shoddy noncompetitive items that everyone else is buying.

Any reasonable person with an open mind readily can see that advertising not only is economically sound, but is essential to maintain and improve our living standards. Standards, it might be added, that are enjoyed to the utmost by many of the nonthinking zealots who would eliminate the advertising that makes them possible.

Some entirely justified criticism is directed at advertising in general when it should be directed to individual advertisers.

Some advertisers, as some gun owners, automobile owners, and printing press owners, do, indeed, use their efforts in ways that should be condemned. But it is as foolish to condemn advertising for the transgressions of a few individuals as it is to condemn the automobile because it is misused, or the printing press because it is occasionally used by counterfeiters.

Advertising serves retailers and manufacturers by spreading the news of goods and services to more people faster at lower cost than any other form of communication.

Advertising serves customers by making possible mass production, which results in lower prices, allowing the purchase of other items, which also are lower priced because of advertising.

SOME BASIC FACTS ABOUT ADVERTISING

You, as a professional in the field of advertising, of which radio advertising is a part, should know the basic facts. Here are some of the most important:

Advertising cannot sell goods or services that people don't want. Many stores waste much of their advertising budgets trying to unload merchandise that never should have been bought. Advertising, used most effectively, informs prospective customers of the availability and benefits of the merchandise. Despite your best motivational efforts, advertising does not create demand in the overall sense. Demand depends upon people's desire to buy as well as their ability to buy. Your expertly written copy can "make 'em want it" and increase sales within certain limits, of course. That's why you write it. But the limits must be recognized.

No matter how carefully contrived your copy, you cannot create demand for Rolls Royce automobiles. The desire to buy already exists but the ability is lacking. Conversely, Chrysler found in the late 30s that little demand could be created for a radical new "airflow" design even though ability to buy, at least comparable to the preceding year, existed. The car was ahead of its time and no appeal was ever found that would convince profitable numbers of people that they wanted it.

Advertising low price alone will not increase demand. That was a lesson learned by buggy whip manufacturers. When an item is ahead or behind fashion or need, advertising is largely wasted on it.

None of these statements in any way negates the example in Chapter 1, which describes the psychology in advertising as a shapeless tube with armholes. In the case of the tube, its time had come. As tasteless as it was, it did conform to current fashion in length, materials, and other details. The tube offered in a Mother Hubbard length would have faced a different fate. Could advertising have sold it? The ready acceptance of some items when first advertised does not demonstrate the ability of advertising to create demand as some people believe. It proves merely that the public is ready for the item.

Perhaps you remember the hula hoop. Following massive TV exposure the hoop swept the country in weeks. Production facilities were operated at capacity. Other facilities were converted to hoop production. Sales increased, and week after week production lagged further behind the orders pouring in from jobbers and wholesalers. It was one of the most profitable and fast-growing fads ever seen in this country. Then it ended.

Could you sell hula hoops in that volume again today? You could not! An effort has been made to revive the fad for a new generation, and it failed. The hula hoop is behind the fashion. Neither massive advertising nor low price will sell it in big volume. The demand does not exist. The hoop is an old-fashioned toy that the parents of today's children played with. They don't want it any more than today's college crowd wants raccoon coats, 1920 style.

Advertising cannot create demand for raccoon coats, buggy whips, hula hoops, and high-button shoes any more than it can create demand for Model T Fords.

Advertising alone will not sell merchandise. The effective and profitable sale of merchandise in retail stores requires intelligent management of the store's overall operation. Where advertising is concerned, this means that other merchandising efforts must be coordinated with the advertising schedule.

Some store managers have "tested" advertising by hiding the advertised merchandise under a counter and counting the number of customers who asked for it. This is like driving your car with the parking brake engaged. Progress is slow and expensive. A small retailer who attempts to test advertising is wasting his time and money foolishly. Advertising has been tested and proven by every conceivable type of business over the last 100 years or so. Radio advertising has been through every imaginable test for more than 40 years. If both advertising and radio were not effective they would have gone down the economic drain many years ago.

Whenever a retailer of whatever size or philosophy invests money in an advertising schedule, one thing is being tested.

That is his merchandising ability. The results depend to a great extent on his skill in selecting merchandise to be advertised, and his efforts to display and sell it in show windows, inside the store, and in other ways such as so-called "free" publicity.

Good advertising that motivates prospects to visit the store is largely wasted unless the advertising is backed up by in-the-store merchandising. A store should advertise only merchandise that reasonably can be expected to move in profitable volume. Except in the case of clearance sales, the merchandise should be new, fresh, and desirable. Then window displays, table or other displays, store posters and other information material should be coordinated to assault the sensibilities of the prospects from all directions at the same time.

Store personnel must be kept informed, trained, and motivated. No matter how successful your advertising copy is in bringing customers into the store, a promotion can be ruined by dull, don't-give-a-damn sales clerks. With a well-coordinated effort the brakes are released and business moves with profitable speed. If the right merchandise is featured and backed up by a complete merchandising plan, it will sell, and sell in profitable quantities.

Advertising must be used continuously for successful results. There is some disagreement as to what constitutes "continuously." Some businesses advertise one day a week. Others advertise seven days a week. Still others advertise one day a month or one week a month. Within the context and requirements of their own businesses, each is advertising continuously. Most retail stores, however, should advertise every week to receive optimum results from their advertising budgets. Advertising, it has been said, is a course of treatment, not a shot in the arm.

Many on-again-off-again retail advertisers argue that customers are already familiar with their stores and merchandise; therefore, advertising would be a waste. This usually is an unconscious admission that the business is so slow-moving that there's nothing new to tell. The reasoning is fallacious.

New people are moving into the community almost daily. Young people are reaching maturity, marrying, and establishing homes constantly. Their interests and needs change as their status changes. Constant advertising is needed to attract these new customers who otherwise may go to other stores. The sometime advertiser has little chance to hold the loyalty of previous customers when his competitors are advertising constantly.

ADVERTISING SERVES CUSTOMERS IN FIVE WAYS

Advertising provides customers with information they need or want. When the spread of information was mostly by word of mouth, the nation was slow to accept bathtubs. As late as 1880, most homes were still without. Today, news of a new faucet design or a new automobile door handle reaches almost every home in the nation within a couple of days.

Advertising assures customers of better merchandise. When a merchant puts his reputation on the line by advertising style, quality, and price, he knows he must deliver what he advertises. He knows his customers must be satisfied with the quality of the product and the integrity of the merchant if they are going to be repeat customers. He must have repeat customers to build and maintain a profitable business.

Advertising makes possible lower prices. The first ball-point pens retailed for about $32, then as mass production resulted from advertising, the price came down to about $12. Further advertising and competition resulting therefrom brought about further refinements in mass production and distribution, reducing costs to the point that today you can buy a ball-point pen for nine cents. If ball-point pen prices had remained static in relation to monetary inflation, a one-dollar pen would carry a price of about $50 today.

Some retailers, usually in out-of-the-way locations, claim to offer lower prices because they don't advertise and, consequently, pass the saving on to their customers. Although an unthinking Mrs. Middle Majority may swallow that without salt, to anyone who is familiar with the basic economics of retailing, it is obviously fallacious.

In the first place they do advertise in various ways—ways that cost substantially. They have large signs outside their stores, show-cards inside, posters inside, handbills delivered to homes, and direct mail—the most expensive cost-per-impression this side of skywriting. A comparison of price and quality usually will reveal that this type of operator deals in inferior merchandise because he cannot take advantage of the economics of mass buying and selling. To compete, he cuts quality as well as price.

The prime point that escapes unthinking customers here is that the advertising cost of one item can hardly be seen. One of the world's largest advertisers is Coca-Cola. A few years ago

Coke's ad budget was said to be $12 million a year. Yet, if the ad budget were completely eliminated from operating expenses the price of a Coke could not be lowered by as much as one cent. The cost of advertising is only a fraction of a cent for each Coca-Cola. The same is true of a pack of cigarettes.

Ad men tell the story of a new, young executive of Coca-Cola who decided to reduce the advertising budget by half and put the $6 million into profit. After six months, sales had slumped to the point that it was necessary to advertise at the rate of $18 million a year to regain Coke's share of the market.

Fortunately, the alternative end to that story was never told. Here is what could have happened had not the advertising budget been restored. If sales had continued to slump, and profits had been curtailed, layoffs would have been made at every local Coca-Cola bottling plant in the country. The cost of producing Coke would have increased, resulting in an increase in the price, further reducing sales and increasing layoffs. Suppliers of glass bottles, bottle caps, wooden crates, delivery trucks, sugar, and other flavoring materials, would have experienced a reduction in sales and, consequently, would have laid off some personnel. The impact of layoffs coast to coast, not only in Coca-Cola plants but in glass plants, bottle cap plants, wood working plants, Detroit's automotive plants, sugar refineries, etc., would have increased the ranks of unemployed.

Unemployment would have drained tax money through welfare and unemployment compensation. The unemployed would have reduced their buying, resulting in decreased sales of almost every product on the American market. Manufacturing operations would have decreased. A new round in the downward spiral of the economy would have resulted from layoffs and reduced retail sales. This would not have been a major recession comparable to one that would be caused by a comparable slump in automobile sales, but it would have been felt in every county in the United States.

The electric light bulb is an example of the cause-and-effect relationship between advertising and lower prices. In 1926 a 60-watt light bulb sold for $1.75. As a result of advertising which increased the number of bulbs needed, the price was reduced to 13 cents in 1942. Such price reductions are the direct result of savings effected by mass production and distribution made possible only by advertising.

Advertising increases the customer's satisfaction with purchases. Most people—especially our target, the middle majority—feel much more satisfaction in wearing and using well-known brands than they do in the purchase of unknown brands. A beginning golfer who is in no way competent to judge one set of clubs against another prefers to buy Spalding, Wilson, or Kroydon clubs rather than the J. C. Higgins brand sold by Sears.

Small town Arkansas girls go to Little Rock to buy expensive fashions; then proudly let their coats hang open to show off the Pfeiffers of Arkansas label. Little Rock girls of more affluent families buy their fashions in New York. Back at home they flaunt their labels from Wannamakers and Lord & Taylor. Entirely apart from satisfactory use of the clothing, they experience enjoyment and satisfaction with the labels.

The satisfaction is a direct result of advertising. Satisfaction comes from the store's reputation. The reputation was built by advertising. The satisfaction is so much a part of the merchandise that a prestige store—especially during the Christmas season—can advertise that "she'll be pleased with any gift that bears the Rich's label."

Advertising makes possible almost universal reception of radio and TV entertainment and wide distribution of newspapers and magazines. Without advertising, the alternative would be for the government to impose a stiff tax on each radio and TV set sold to finance government-owned stations, as is the policy in England. Without advertising a typical small-town weekly newspaper, if such existed at all, would retail at prices ranging from 50 cents to a dollar. Metropolitan dailies would sell for considerably more, national magazines for several dollars.

Now, with the necessity of advertising in view, let's consider copy approaches useful in promoting sales of typical products.

AIR CONDITIONING

Motivation: Happiness, comfort, snobbery

Key idea: Cool comfort

Residential air conditioning has become a virtual necessity to upper and middle class existence in many areas of the United States. It is now in a situation similar to that of automobiles and boats. Bigger, better, and more luxurious air conditioning is desirable as a symbol of status.

Like a young couple who starts with a Falcon and over the years trades up to a Cadillac, owners of air conditioning units may start with one window unit, add others one or two at a time, and soon find that their goal is not mere cool comfort, but a central air conditioning system. It may be installed in the present home, or may be a strong motivation to buy or build a new home.

Motivational research has revealed that many people find a hidden degree of security in air conditioners and are susceptible to an appeal based on keeping the house sealed against dirt, dust, pollen, and other "threatening" things while they sleep. Psychiatrists say that keeping the house sealed against "threats" stems from a desire for more security. The copy should stress cool comfort, enjoyment, entertaining in luxurious coolness (implying that it equals if not surpasses that of the entertainees) and family happiness. Appeals that apply to houses also have some application to anything that becomes a part of household living.

Helpful words and phrases

heavy duty	big	easy
luxury	delightful coolness	furniture styled
carefree	engineered	powerful
	quiet	

Luxury of really big cooling power

Satisfying cooling power

Quiet power of satisfying coolness

Serene satisfaction

The satisfaction of a quiet, powerful coolness

Live, relax, entertain, in luxurious coolness that keeps you always at your best.

Get away from it all this summer—in the luxurious coolness of your home.

Feel like the woman you are in the luxurious coolness of your own home.

The cool serenity of your own personality

Luxurious coolness that enhances the warm glow of your own personality

You'll always be at your charming best, whether you're relaxing with your family or having friends in for dinner.

APARTMENT RENTAL

Motivation: Security, esteem, wealth, snobbery, comfort, safety

Key idea: Enjoyable living

A consideration of recent years is "safety in numbers." Apartment dwellers can leave town for a weekend or vacation, or a man can work late, knowing that the apartment management will keep an eye on things. Burglary, thievery, or vandalism is a concern of management.

Consideration of neighbors as individuals and friends is not vital, but "swinging singles" prefer to be among their own type, as do executives, constant socializers, etc. More basic considerations are the same as those involved in houses. A woman tends to view her home as an extension of her own personality. A man is likely to view it as a refuge from abrasions of the outside world. A "good" address, convenience to schools, shopping, office, or other work sites are strong selling points.

Helpful words and phrases

spacious	secluded	delightful
convenient	charming	traditional
atmosphere	handsome	gracious
modern	tasteful	practical
enjoyable		

If your address is important

An address of distinction

Just a few minutes from everywhere

Note: See "Houses" for further suggestions.

AUTOMOBILES

Motivation: Pride of ownership, esteem, security, sex

Key idea: Size and luxury, plus local dealer's own appeals

Pride of ownership based on size and luxury is the strongest appeal. Research has revealed that it is a woman's desire to "ride in it," be seen in it by friends and neighbors, and a man's desire to "take care of it," much as a woman cares for a home. Advertising appeal for Ford's Maverick includes the suggestion that "you can change the spark plugs" and do other minor mechanical jobs on it.

Pitch your auto copy, both new and used, to the enjoyment of a new standard of luxury, even if that new standard is merely upgrading from a 10-year-old Ford to an 8-year-old Ford. Virtually every auto dealer in town is advertising "the lowest price" or "the best deal," but what a car buyer wants—even though he does accept the auto industry's open invitation to chisel on prices—is the emotional satisfaction of owning a newer, bigger, and more prestigious car.

The wife is definitely influential in determining the type and color of a family car. A young unmarried man is influenced by what he believes to be the car's effect on his image in the eyes of girls. Power is an ever-present factor in a car-buyer's mind. Most men consider more power to be desirable in and of itself, but the belief must be rationalized by concepts of an extra margin of safety which results from the unnecessary power. Research has shown that for many men, high speed is a means of letting off aggressive feelings, something never admitted, but which is an important factor in automobile advertising.

Other research indicates that a new and more powerful car tends to renew a man's sense of power and to reassure him of his own powerful masculinity. That renewed feeling, of course, wears off and a year or two later another new car is required to recharge his subconscious battery. The new "muscle" cars and their projected progeny are aimed directly at that target.

Helpful phrases

Enjoy the smooth feel of BIG power.

Test drive it; enjoy the true luxury of handsome fittings and all the options.

Zoom right up to a new standard of driving enjoyment.

Put yourself in the seat of power; you'll find it big, luxurious, and perfect for a fast-moving man who gets things done.

If you're the type of man who wants plenty of power under your foot...

You'll enjoy the smooth feel of real luxury in downtown traffic, and out on the highway you can let go with man-size power.

King-size power on the highway; queen-size control downtown

AUTO ACCESSORIES

Motivation: Esteem, security, snobbery, acquisitiveness

Key idea: Your car says something about who you are.

Auto accessories are bought almost exclusively by men. There is a definite parallel between a man's attitude toward his car and his home. There is an element of security involved in a man's attachment to his car. There he is his own boss, master of his rolling universe, captain of his ship, the king of his chromed castle. The car is his security blanket.

Can the king be blamed for decreeing more class, more comfort, more convenience, more conspicuous enjoyment of the most expensive (at least the second most expensive) thing he owns? A pair of fuzzy little "goof balls" or giant-size polyfoam dice hanging from the rear-view mirror is to him the equivalent of a rhinestone necklace with matching earrings for his mate. A pair of dummy spotlights may give him the same sense of "being somebody" that an overly elaborate and overly expensive barbecue grill would give his gray flannel counterpart in another neighborhood.

Auto accessories for the most part are sold purely for the purpose of emotional satisfaction. A service station operator who deals widely in auto accessories was observed buying a station-wagon load of merchandise at a wholesale accessory house. In the $600 order were only two items, retailing for about $25 each, that conceivably could serve a useful function in an automobile. The other items were purely decorative.

To the type of man who is a prospect for such items, his car is a place to plant a duplicate of himself as a woman does in her home. While most people tend to buy cars that "say something" about their personalities, an accessory prospect completes the circle by impressing his own personality on the car. A foxtail or colored ball flying from the radio antenna says something about the owner. It also constitutes a message from the owner to all who see him.

It is comparable to the special purpose flags hoisted by yacht owners. When the sun is over the yard arm, up goes the flag showing a cocktail glass. Both the foxtail and the cocktail glass say to the world that "here is a free spirit, a fun lover, enjoying life. Watch me, folks, here I go, enjoying living. Wheee."

The same type of young man who first invests in a foxtail, or drives into a service station for a free plastic antenna banana, is a prime prospect for custom seat covers to hide the beautiful and carefully designed upholstery perfected for his car. He's a sucker for a pitch to cover the luxurious carpeting with rubber floor mats, thereby "saving" the carpeting for a higher trade-in value. It takes very little suggestion to convince him that his standard license plate, identical in material and design to every other license plate of his state, needs the special protection of a chrome-framed glass cover. All it takes to sell him a pair of totally nonfunctional dummy spotlights is to point out that he really can afford it if he wants to. A key with ornate head and different—if not better—key ring or case to hold it are bought in a moment. A decal picturing a "road runner" or a bumper strip with comic comment is decided on in seconds.

Anything that stamps a facet of the owner's personality on the car is eagerly accepted. It's as desirable as more horse-power. He buys such brick-a-brack as compulsively as some women buy costume jewelry. To sell auto accessories, use the image of a man who is proud of his car, who enjoys caring for his car, and who has an abundance of worldly knowledge. The prospect likes to feel that he is sophisticated and capable of handling any situation that may arise. In truth, his sophistication has little relation to that found in the pages of Esquire, Playboy, and Fortune.

Helpful phrases

The man with a go-go attitude

For the man who stays out in front

For the man who knows what a car is for

The man who cares for his car

The dashing look

The hot car look for the man who plays it cool

Say something about yourself

This side of the generation gap

Makes your car part of you

BARGAIN DEPARTMENT STORES

Motivation: Wealth, plus various others

Key idea: Save money on the things you need.

The bargain store is usually of the type known as a "junior department store." It is found in every small town, as well as larger cities, and depends on well-promoted "sales" about every other week for the majority of its business. Sale merchandise traditionally is seconds and irregulars. Such chains as Belk's, B. C. Moore & Sons, Wests, and Dollar General Stores are typical of the type. They are and have been heavy users of radio. Usually, the smaller the market the larger slice of the budget that goes into radio.

Typical customers for such promotion store sales are those at the lower end of the sophistication scale who can be stampeded into "rushing right down" to buy "sensational bargains throughout the store." This type of store manager tends to equate a one-minute spot with half a newspaper page and unless he receives some beneficial education from station personnel, is likely to demand that a list of 10 or 12 bargain-priced items be listed in each 60-second spot.

Four items are about the most that can be handled effectively. Of those four, one should be given prominence and really sold with solid motivation. The other three, then, can be mentioned as additional bargains among the tremendous array, etc.

The principle of featuring one item and using the others to support the idea of the sale was crystallized many years ago by designers of newspaper front pages. You'll notice that the principle is applied every day. A good editor knows that nothing on the page should fight for attention with his leading headline and story. By the same reasoning, no two or more bargains should fight for dominance in your copy. To allow equal emphasis for two items is to detract from the impact of each.

Copy should give an overall impression of the exciting money-saving event, implying that there is much, much more than can be described or mentioned in a short time. Thrust of the effort should be to make the prospect want to go to the store and shop all departments, while promoting one specific item as an example, with two or three other items as supporting evidence of the wide selection of breath-taking bargains. J. C. Penney Co. provides transcribed commercials that are excellent examples of this type of copy.

Helpful words and phrases

spectacular values	lovely	vivid
fantastic	today	striking
tremendous	thrifty prices	practical
marvelous	fine quality	delightful
fabulous	fashion-right	alluring price
exquisite	money-saving	wonderful buys
extraordinary	long-lasting	this season's
quality	long-wearing	going fast
beautiful	gorgeous	hurry

The price on this one is only...

Save dollars at this low, low price of only...

Made to sell for

Gorgeous dresses at a fraction of their usual price

They won't last long

Tagged at only $8.99

BANKS

Motivation: Complex, reaching into every facet of life

Key idea: The bank is friendly and helpful

As late as 1958, a public opinion survey showed that the vast majority of people in the United States tended to view bankers as stuffed shirts. This image of a banker, looking down in pompous disapproval, is the obstacle that virtually all bank advertising today is designed to overcome.

Many banks advertise that they are "full service" banks and then promote each service separately. Others, not providing full service, take the same approach, merely omitting any mention of "full service," which is rather meaningless to most listeners.

Underlying all your bank copy should be the theme of friendly help. The services offered by a bank are promoted separately: savings, home loans, auto loans, home improvement loans, real estate loans, business expansion loans, income tax loans, safe deposit boxes, insurance department, trust department, etc. Each service should be offered as "help" to your listener. He is inclined to view a banker as one who disapproves of his money management. To overcome that barrier, the theme of "friendly" should be stressed without sounding phony. (One bank, to be different as well as realistic, advertises that it is "almost friendly.") Dialogue copy, recorded by competent talent and using jingles with a happy sound, generally is most effective, although there have been as many successful approaches to advertising for banks as for other types of business.

BOATS

Motivation: Happiness, esteem

Key idea: Conspicuous enjoyment

Boat ownership is a symbol of status. At the lower end of the boat owner scale is a hard-core group of fishermen who use relatively small and inexpensive boats. In the absence of boats, these men (and women) would have to fish from the banks and bridges.

Generally, the boat owner is concerned with size and luxury in the same manner and for the same reasons he is concerned with the same characteristics in his automobile. Here, it may be assumed that the lady of the house wants to "ride in it" and be seen enjoying the luxury by friends, neighbors, and acquaintances. The man wants to take care of it as he cares for his car. Both want the status—esteem—that comes from owning a boat, perhaps the only one in the neighborhood, or at least a larger, more luxurious and better cared-for boat than any of the others.

162

When it comes to buying a cruiser or houseboat with living accommodations, a prospect is vulnerable to some of the same hidden motivations that send him house hunting. A man is likely to look on it as a place to get away from abrasions of the business world. A woman wants to put the imprint of her personality on it by decorating it, buying or making draperies, selecting carpets, colors, and accessories. Copy should emphasize size, luxury, convenience, liveability. As with automobiles, financing is a major concern and your copy should stress the ease with which it may be arranged.

Except in the case of a serious sports fisherman, a pleasure boat owner rarely has any urgent destination. Nevertheless, power is important to him just as it is on the highway. The hidden motivation is the unconscious drive to feel more powerful as he roars idly across the lake or up the river, ever striving to get nowhere faster. Availability of service and mechanical parts is a practical consideration. A fiberglass hull that never needs painting is a valuable plus, not only from a financial viewpoint, but in convenience as well.

The primary motivation for buying a boat is to enhance the owner's happiness, whether he's fishing, cruising, or just hiding from the world. However, as is the case with the automobile dealer, it is necessary to use appeals associated with your client to distinguish him from other boat dealers in the area, rather than depending on merely selling the brand of boat.

Helpful words and phrases

big	engineered	dashing
wide	sleek	long
convenient	powerful	comfortable
distinctive	smooth	enjoyable
luxurious	designed	luxuriate

fast

Surging power that gets you there and back—faster

You can feel the smooth surge of power as you move the throttle all the way—up to a roaring 35 knots.

A big boat, a luxurious boat, yet easily mounted on its trailer and stored in your backyard between outings

Invite your friends aboard and listen to their envious conpliments.

It's decorated handsomely to invite compliments.

But there's room for the play of your own creative imagination as you add personal accessories to make it distinctively yours.

Years of nautical research and experimentation have at last brought you the ultimate in size, luxury and all 'round enjoyability in a $3,500 boat.

BOOKS

Motivation: Happiness, enjoyment, acquisitiveness, snobbery

Key idea: A memorable experience

Note: These comments apply to books for the general market, novels and nonfiction intended for entertainment or general enlightenment. With a few exceptions, such as educational materials, books are mostly bought for one basic reason. The reader wants to enjoy a **memorable experience**.

Books usually are promoted one at a time rather than in a listing like much other merchandise. Radio is rarely used, but a demonstration of effective copy could change that situation. (A national advertising agency has reported gratifying success in promoting a new dictionary with radio.)

Novels and exposes offer dramatic possibilities of strong emotional appeals very much like movie advertising. Present the book as a vitally enjoyable experience, appealing to as many emotions as you reasonably can. Use strong words, strong statements. Emphasize the various emotions the prospect will experience: shocking, revealing, unbelievable, staggering, charming, delightful, breezy, zany, hilarious, magnificent, inspiring.

The use of strong words and strong statements, positive statements, accomplishes the same thing in the mind of your listener as the preliminary statements of a hypnotist. They prepare your listener to experience what you want her (or him) to experience. It's like a photographer in older days who sensitized his own plates by coating them with a light-sensitive emulsion. Later he inserted the plate into his camera and opened the lens, letting in light reflected from the subject, thereby etching the subject's image in the emulsion. Your strong statements, your strong words painting a picture of the emotions you expect your listener to experience in reading the book, have the effect of sensitizing her mind to those very same emotions.

Not only does she feel (and that is the correct word, **feel**) the desirability of reading the book, she actively expects to experience the emotions you describe. Then when she reads, she does, in fact, experience them, usually more intensely than if she had not been prepared for the experience. Put your prospect right into the picture; get her itching to start reading. "You'll turn page after page in unbelieving amazement as the shocking story unfolds." The use of appropriate music in production offers many effective possibilities, too.

Inspirational and how-to books have essentially the same appeal; that is, a how-you-too-can-improve-your-life appeal. Tell your listener how much better she will be or how much more she can accomplish, how her status will improve, how much more she will get out of or enjoy life. Emphasize the fact, "release the tremendous powers within you" or "gain the serene relief from petty frustrations that allows you to rise above the nagging clamor of every-day life" or make friends faster, zoom to a higher income, live in comfort and luxury; be the envy of your friends when you produce professional quality flower arrangements for your home, your church, and civic affairs. One key principle in selling how-to books is this: It is far more effective to sell "release the power **already** within you" than to suggest that much study and hard work will be needed.

If time permits, appeal to the physical senses:

Sight: This handsome, red, Morocco-like cover with gorgeous gold lettering...

Touch: Has the rich, luxurious feel of quality

In the case of inspirational and how-to books—especially inspirational—the experience wanted is not simply the reading, but an experience of some kind of improvement expected to follow the reading. In the case of novels and exposes, as well as other factual books on current affairs, the reader expects to experience immediate emotion while reading.

DECOR

Motivation: Esteem

Key idea: Charm, gracious atmosphere

Home decor is a wide field embracing departments in furniture, variety, and gift shops as well as department stores.

It includes such widely divergent items as carpets, ash trays, lamps, and wall hangings ranging from 98-cent framed prints to oriental tapestries. The **one idea** to remember is that a woman buying decorating items is extending her personality to another physical area of her home. Ideas of what constitutes a charming, gracious atmosphere are as diverse as women's personalities.

Here are some guidelines that may be helpful:

Better educated persons tend to prefer muted and neutral colors, depending upon an occasional strong accent. Relatively unschooled people tend to favor brilliant colors such as red and orange. The dividing line, color engineering specialists have discovered, depends on available emotional outlets. People with many emotional outlets (usually better educated) favor the muted colors.

Rooms decorated in accordance with the tastes of the executive and professional class tend to repel the mass-market prospects. And vice versa. One research firm put a class label on some items. The knickknack shelf is likely to be found in lower-class homes; Venetian blinds in the upper middle; and solid-color carpets in the upper class.

Helpful words and phrases

Check and evaluate those suggested for both Fashion and Houses. Some are related to the extension of a woman's personality, graciousness and charm.

DISCOUNT STORES

Motivation: Wealth, plus others

Key Idea: Save money on a wide variety of things you need.

For discount houses the techniques are virtually the same as those used for Bargain Department Store copy. Here it may be assumed that the merchandise is first quality unless the client tells you otherwise. The discount is justified by quantity buying. One chain, headquartered in Dallas, is comprised mostly of franchised stores, but agreements with suppliers specify that individual stores may buy independently at a 10 percent discount. Similar buying practices exist in various forms in all chains.

Helpful words and phrases

See Bargain Department Stores

DRUG STORES

Motivation: Various

Key idea: Wide variety of things you need are found in one convenient location.

Specific items advertised may be bargains or they may be a regular price line of staple items. Generally, the best copy for a drug store builds the image of wide variety, complete selections, helpful service, and convenient location, while promoting one specific item or class of items.

Traditionally, drug stores have received their revenue in about equal portions from prescriptions, merchandise, and the soda fountain. Today's trend is toward the elimination of fountains because of labor costs and allied problems.

Drug store owners tend to favor advertising prescriptions over the other two departments. This appears to be an unwarranted prejudice, but no information is available to make a definite conclusion.

Drug stores often have coop advertising allowances, especially for vitamins, but also for hard merchandise. If coop specifications permit, it is good practice to work at your task of building the store image as you promote specific items.

Drug stores generally enjoy slightly better than average business in July and October and do a whopping 11 percent of their year's business in December.

Helpful words and phrases

convenient	famous brands	enjoyable atmosphere
wide selection	carefully compounded	spacious
quality	nationally known	right down town

DRY CLEANERS
(and laundry)

Motivation: Esteem, convenience

Key idea: Make your clothes look like new.

This service is a staple pretty much taken for granted, a necessity that is bought usually as a routine. Pickup and delivery service is convenient and desirable when a household has some one available to deal with the driver.

For working couples, a convenient location passed on normal trips to and from work is a strong selling point.

Price, compared to a competitor with comparable locations, is an important consideration. But slightly higher price is no obstacle when compared to the necessity of driving several blocks out of the way during rush hours to save 20 cents. Average middle income prospects are likely to say, "taint worth it."

A location is convenient only in relation to specific prospects. A shop convenient to prospects on the west side can be completely out of the question for prospects on the east side of a city of 30,000 or more.

Your copy should show the personal enjoyment and other benefits (business and social) of keeping clothing in the best possible condition. Dramatize the brand new look of freshly cleaned and pressed or laundered clothing.

EMPLOYMENT AGENCIES

Motivation: Happiness, sex, wealth, security

Key idea: A better, more enjoyable life

Employment agency business is booming. Once limited to markets of 100,000 or more, offices are now opening in cities as small as 15,000. The business is based on promotion. An employment agency must advertise consistently, every week, usually every day.

Traditionally, they have been limited to dull but practical newspaper classified sections. A combination of top-notch professionally conceived copy and a station manager with vision to see the possibilities has broken the tradition in several markets. Basic to selling them on radio is an understanding of two factors:

A. Economics of the business

B. Motivation of applicants

The economics are simple: fees from applicants who accept jobs resulting from the agency's efforts range from about 7 percent of the first year's pay to about 15 percent. Fees are determined by a sliding scale. There appears to be little standardization of scales.

In most agencies, the counselor, who deals directly with both the applicant and the employer, gets one-third of the fee upon payment. The contract with the applicant usually specifies payment within 30 days. Two-thirds goes to the agency to cover expenses and profit.

Most independent agencies operate with one to three counselors and have little, if any, desire to expand. Franchised agencies, and an occasional growth-minded local independent, engage in continuous high-pressure sales management. The carrot and stick technique is used extensively.

Relatively small rewards are offered counselors for such achievements as: most applications taken, most applicants sent to interviews, most employers brought to the agency for series of interviews, etc. Substantial cash bonuses are offered for exceeding placement quotas, which result, of course, in giant leaps of gross income.

Typical fee for placing an applicant in a $100-a-week job is $300. The counselor, who handles it all, gets $100. If other employment agency offices are involved in either recruiting the applicant or referring him to a successful job interview, there is a more complex split.

Motivation of applicants varies with the type of agency. General agencies handle all comers. Specialized agencies handle applicants for such fields as accounting and finance; sales and marketing; hotel and restaurant, etc. The general agency, dealing mostly in jobs for office girls, is by far the best prospect, although a sales and marketing specialist could benefit greatly from well-conceived radio advertising.

General agencies are excellent prospects for two reasons. First, applicants in these days of booming economy are far harder for an agency to come by than are potential employers. Agencies have many more job orders than they can fill. Any time they can get a half-way qualified office girl they can place her.

Second, the agency can create turnover, which otherwise would not occur, by motivating girls who are already satisfactorily employed to change jobs. This is done by using the basic technique of offering more than the physical merchandise. The merchandise in this case is a job virtually identical to the applicant's present job. The difference between the prospect's present job and the job in which an agency can place her is the difference between Ford and Chevrolet, the difference between a Van Heusen shirt and a Manhattan shirt. The difference is image. Nothing more.

The image of a new job is made attractive by lacing it with the possibility of romance. A single girl resists that appeal like an alcoholic resists a Christmas gift of Kentucky bourbon. Copy is directed to the point that "while nobody knows who you'll meet when you change jobs, he could be a handsome, high-paid executive who frequently travels to exotic lands, drives a T-Bird, owns a cruiser on the lake, and is excitingly single." Your copy should be more subtle than this explanation, but the blatant pitch for romance can be effective.

A long campaign, conceivably, could use many other appeals directed toward specific businesses (airline recruiters use world travel as a carrot) but for recruiting single girls, nothing will beat romance.

FARM IMPLEMENTS

Motivation: Wealth, security, esteem

Key idea: Faster, better farm work at reduced costs of time and labor

There are three reasons a businessman buys equipment or supplies for his business:

1. To make money

2. To save money

3. To do a better job

A businessman in the field of farming has the same basic interests. His wardrobe may contain more bib overalls than gray flannel suits, but his problems in deciding whether to buy implements and other hardware are the same as those of a factory manager.

His greatest problem is the high cost of labor. A machine to increase the amount of work one employe can do is worth money to him. It will help pay for itself every hour it is used. Every farm implement is designed to appeal to one or more of the three above motivations.

The same appeals apply to renting equipment or contracting for specific work on the farm. The average farmer would not buy a bulldozer because he probably doesn't need it more than one or two weeks a year. It is more economical to rent it or contract to have a professional dirt mover do the work.

A pickup truck, psychologically, is not a farm implement but an automobile. Consequently, it is subject to all the irrational motivations that sell automotive merchandise. This explains the development of nonfunctional body styling and bright 2-tone finishes. It is likely that your farm implement dealers do their biggest business in April, May, June and July.

FASHIONS

Motivation: Esteem and sex

Key idea: Beautiful appearance

A woman is most likely to favor "this year's styles and colors" over any practical considerations such as suitability to her own shape or coloring. Whether she's buying a waitress' uniform or an elegant evening gown for the president's ball, she wants to know that it conforms to the tastes of **today**. She is likely to buy a dress that she knows is less flattering to her because of the "in" color or styling, rather than one that is more suited to her but lacks some obvious clue that ties it to current fashion.

A suggestion that a wise choice of fashion **now** will produce manifestations of jealous envy in other girls, if handled with taste (and perhaps wit), is effective. Remember that **most** women have little intellectual foundation on which to form their own tastes and **must** depend on flamboyant "leaders" and communications media for determination as to what is "right." A rack of utterly tasteless dresses can be glamorized and made highly desirable overnight by the appearance in a movie, TV show, or newspaper picture of a skinny, supercilious jet setter wearing a similar item.

This principle applies, of course, to all women's fashions—shorts, slacks, swim suits, hair bands, blouses, bras, garter belts, and bobby pins. The workings of the principle are even more pronounced among younger teenagers, to whom nonconformity is social death.

Your women's wear clients are likely to do their biggest business in October, November, and December, with the year's low point coming in January and February. December, alone, accounts for about 15 percent of the year's business in the average women's wear shop or department.

Helpful words and phrases

beautiful	today's	snappy	wonderful
dashing	charming	pert	smart
graceful	light	lush	perky
splendor	polished	captivating	fanciful
harmonious	magnificent	airy	delightful

tidy	bright	brilliant	elegant
fresh	neat	exquisite	radiant
glossy	resplendent	vivid	delicate
grand	sleek	spruce	sparkling
formal	classic	dazzling	jaunty
conventional	informal	rich	glowing
gorgeous	distinguished	attractive	superb
bright	lovely	casual	precise
practical			simplicity

Brings out the real you

Float along (or walk, move, relax, etc.) in the breath of spring

The essence of loveliness (or charm or beauty)

Give your own personality free rein to charm and captivate in this stunning...

Lush and lovely

Wide and wonderful selection

Free and fanciful

Makes you feel like the woman you are

FLOOR COVERINGS

Motivation: Esteem, security

Key idea: A more luxurious home

Floor coverings include carpets, rugs, throw rugs, linoleum and similar hard-finish materials. The difference between a carpet and a rug is that a rug is movable; a carpet is wall-to-wall. The distinction is easily overlooked and is not highly important to most prospects. But the difference should be noted and carefully observed in copy.

Floor coverings are an integral part of a residence, be it house or apartment, so the same motivations and helpful

172

words and phrases apply. Notice that a home is visualized by a man as a place of refuge, to get away from the abrasions of the outside world. A woman is likely to view it as an extension of her own personality.

Strong rainbow colors are most likely to appeal to lower and the lower middle income groups. It has been revealed by motivational research that a person's color preference is determined by the number of emotional outlets he has. A woman who holds an office in a garden club or other civic organization; who writes occasionally for the organization publication; plays piano for her own pleasure; teaches one of her children the rudiments of art; entertains frequently, and is a member of a bridge club is more likely to prefer the muted colors. A woman whose chief activities are housework and TV watching is likely to prefer strong colors. Also, she is likely to prefer a design which includes flowers rather than any geometric or other abstract design.

Floor coverings of the hard-finished type are subject to the same emotional appeals as rugs and carpets but have a different sales pattern. While carpet departments do less than average monthly business in April and May, the hard-finished floor covering advertiser does better-than average business. He is likely to do about 9.5 percent of his business in October and still hold his sales above average in November. The carpet advertiser's peak business is more likely to peak in September, October and November.

FLYING SCHOOL

Motivation: Happiness, esteem, sex

Key idea: Learn to fly; it's the greatest thing that'll ever happen to you.

This motivation is as complex as that involved with automobiles. There are elements of sex, aggression, acquisitiveness, snobbery, and endless other less definable feelings that go into the desire to fly. A prospect who has the latent motivation, of whatever origin, is likely to catch fire at his first exposure to flying in a small plane.

Most prospects no more know wh they want to fly than they know why they want to drive or smoke. Some businessmen students are first motivated by a real need for faster, more convenient transportation. But as they investigate the possibilities, their motivations become more complex and emotional, tied to the power, esteem, and exhiliration they get from flying.

There is an element of bandwagon psychology in the desire to learn to fly. Once exposed to the enjoyment and potential control of all that roaring power, the ability to go sailing off into the wild and blue, at first alone and then with admiring passengers, the prospect gets caught up in a new world. Private flying (known as General Aviation) is one of the fastest growing businesses in the world. A prospect soon learns this at the first exposure and feels that it would be intolerable to live out his life without the many benefits of personal flying.

There is literally no limit to the number of potential prospects for a flying school operator. The key to increasing his business in dramatic leaps lies in your ability to motivate the right people—men women and teenagers—to go into his establishment and expose themselves to the possibility.

Among the benefits

1. Planes can be rented by the day, mile, hour, month, or year by qualified and licensed private pilots.

2. Planes can be bought new for as little as $7,500, with the most popular single-engine craft running about $12,000 to $15,000, depending on optional radio equipment.

3. A plane can be bought, rented, or leased for business purposes and most of the cost charged against legitimate business expenditure, while it is available for a considerable amount of personal and family enjoyment.

4. A nonbusiness pilot can own or rent a plane for pleasure. He can quit work in Nashville a little early on Friday afternoon, pile the family into a 4-place plane, and be on a beach in the Florida panhandle before dark; it's a 12-to-15 hour drive by car. He could just as easily make his destination Chicago, or Hot Springs. His gasoline expense will be less than if he had driven a 6-cylinder Chevrolet.

5. Football games, stock car races in Atlanta, Darlington, and Daytona Beach, hockey playoffs, world series, and hunting and fishing camps are common targets for private pilots. On long vacation trips of a thousand miles or more flying gives both flexibility and speed, allowing more time in more places.

Among the psychological benefits:

1. An even greater feeling of power than experienced in driving a car.

2. Unparalleled freedom, known only to pilots

3. The thrill of speed, cruising at speeds of 100 to 120 mph in most single-engine craft

4. The esteem of envious associates

Both Cessna and Piper have effective national advertising programs designed to motivate prospects to move. Local advertising by aviation services, which usually includes teaching, sales, and service, is generally very poor and is generally limited to newspapers and telephone directories. Local advertising is mostly of a directory nature, for people already interested in learning to fly.

Present advertising rarely does anything to motivate. You can improve on it with a well-planned campaign designed to bring entirely new prospects into contact with flying school operators. Economics are in your favor. Prices for the entire private license course range from $535 to $650 or more, depending on location and facilities. One sale justifies substantial advertising. A continuing campaign that results in three or four sales a week would be one of the greatest things that ever happened to a small or medium-market flying school operator.

Helpful words and phrases

1. A freedom that you've never known before

2. The freest feeling you'll ever know

3. Power, speed, freedom, the essence of today's leaders

4. Power, speed, freedom—what it takes to be a leader in today's world

5. Makes you feel like the man you are

6. The world looks up to a man who flies

7. You get away from it all—FAST—when you're the pilot.

8. You're in control when you're the pilot.

9. You control it all when you're the pilot—power, speed, and the freedom to go when and where you wish.

10. Live with power; live with speed; live the freest life you've ever known.

11. The world stands still. The world stands still for you. The world stands still for you when you're the pilot looking down from 10,000 feet.

12. You get a masterful view of the world.

13. The troubles you face here on earth look a lot smaller when you're big enough to look down on them from 10,000 feet.

14. You feel so much bigger when you look down on the world from 10,000 feet.

15. The butcher, the baker, the candlestick maker—everybody's flying, including the bright young man on his way up.

mastery	free	take charge	fun
zoom	powerful	future	control
masterful	flexible	travel	modern
speed	bright	leader	respect
power	space-age	growing	direct

FURNITURE

Motivation: Security, snobbery, acquisitiveness

Key idea: Charm

The motivation to purchase furniture is directly related to maintaining the security of the home. A woman is likely to look on her home as an extension of her personality and to a man his home is a comfortable refuge from abrasions of the outside world.

There are two basic types of furniture: One is modern, or contemporary, as it is called. It is designed of today's materials for today's environment. The key word in the design (not motivation) is functional. Modern furniture is functional because, in theory, every element of the design performs a useful furniture function, rather than merely being decorative. Modern furniture appeals almost exclusively to the executive and professional class. They are more inclined to think for themselves and form their own ideas about the reasons for furniture design.

The other type of furniture is divided into many styles, but all of them depend upon designs that were created for times that are now history. The designs were created originally by designers and craftsmen as **modern** for their times. The designs were uniquely suited to the home environment, the attitude of the times, the available materials, and the then modern tools.

Original Early American, French Provincial, Spanish, Mediterranean, as well as the classic Chippendale and Duncan Phyfe styles were perfectly suited to their times and places. Today their appeal is based on the "charm" which derives from association with supposedly gracious days of old. There also is an element of security in a woman's choice of older styles which have achieved wide acceptance. She is relying on the judgment of other people, judgment that has been honored by much imitation over many years.

A woman wants furniture that adds charm in a manner that is consistent with her own view of her personality. At the same time she is more likely to be concerned with creating an impression that her husband is a success than in solving any basic problems of decor. It is likely that she also is attempting to show that her knowledgeable taste is a cut above that of her neighbors.

Snobbery, the attitude that "it's up to the Joneses to keep up with us," is a strong factor affecting the choice of store more than the choice of furniture. The wife of a bank president or of a university chancellor is unlikely to buy **anything** from a store whose slogan is "the working man's friend." But a truck driver's wife might bypass the working man's friend to buy from a store known to cater to the white collar trade.

Helpful words and phrases

charm	handsome	soft	solid
approval	deep	delightful	comfortable
sparkle	atmosphere	carefree	airy
tradition	dramatic	practical	elegance
neat	dignity	old world	convenient
softness	luxurious	warmth	continental

The unmistakable warmth of natural wood

The warmth and charm of genuine cherry (pecan or walnut)

As new as tomorrow's sunrise

Created for today's decor

Seems to imbue any room with the charm and dignity of provincial France (or Spain).

Choose this fine traditional design of simplicity and charm to harmonize with your own personality.

Extend the glow of your own personality throughout your entire home

Delightful simplicity of the modern look

Designed with today's materials for today's living

The warm and cozy look of Early American

The wonderfully complex designs of old Spain (or provincial France or the sunny Mediterranean)

Elegance, dignity and charm

Traditional elegance combined with the look of today

The elegance of yesterday; the practicality of today

Create an atmosphere of traditional dignity and charm that immediately tells every visitor that this is where you live.

The convenience of luxury

The luxury of convenience

Choose this look of the sunny Mediterranean and prepare for the flood—the flood of compliments from your friends, neighbors, and relatives.

Even your mother-in-law will approve your choice.

Comfortable convenience for your family today

An atmosphere with the distinctive influence of your own personality

Create an atmosphere that immediately tells every visitor that here is a modern family living in comfort and happiness.

An atmosphere that sparkles with luxury, comfort and happiness.

If the appearance of your living room is important to you...

Create a dramatic atmosphere of gracious hospitality.

Real deep down comfort and gracious hospitality

A delightful atmosphere of traditional charm that makes you feel like the woman you are.

Nothing says so much about the way you live as the way you dine.

Simple elegance

If you like to entertain in an atmosphere of (pick an adjective) elegance

Furniture stores normally do the most business in December, with October and November close to the peak. Lowest month for the average furniture dealer is January. His business tends to build steadily to October, drop very slightly (less than one percent) in November, and finish the year with a satisfying 10.5 percent for December.

HARDWARE STORES

Motivation: Widely variable, but security is a common denominator.

Key idea: Variable, depending on what is advertised. Some hardware stores advertise specific items. Others advertise the store as a place to buy a wide variety of items.

Coop allowance is usually the store manager's motivation for advertising appliances. The customer's motivations for buying are the same as for homes and furniture. They have their basis in security, snobbery, and other considerations involved with home ownership.

For copy promoting the store or specific types of merchandise, such as building hardware, home conveniences, electrical supplies, etc., two principle motivations apply: convenience and acquisitiveness. A good hardware store may stock more items than a good supermarket. It is one of the most difficult retail businesses to learn thoroughly. A typical hardware store does about 12.5 percent of its business in

December and about nine percent in each of the months of June, October, and November. February is the low month with about six percent.

HOUSES

Motivation: For women, fulfillment

For men, refuge

Basic to both, happiness

Key ideas: Your home is your kingdom.

A woman sees her home as an extension of her own personality. She plants and grows a sort of duplication of herself. Men tend to identify home with the security they knew at home as a child. To a man it is likely to be a refuge from the abrasions of the outside world. Generally, it is more effective to pitch copy either to women or to men, but not both at the same time, although it is possible that an especially astute copywriter can incorporate both types of appeal in the same copy.

Helpful words and phrases

spacious	neat	gracious	luxurious
tasteful	convenient	modern	practical
calm	charming	secluded	handsome
traditional	delightful	contemporary	designed

Tastefully modern   The right address

Happy family life   Gracious tradition

Desirable address   If your address is important

The address of your family's future

If where you live is important

If it matters where you live

Timeless taste of gracious traditional design

MEN'S CLOTHING

Motivation: Esteem, sex

Key idea: Good appearance

About half of all men's suits and more than two-thirds of men's shirts sold are bought by women. There is a school of thought which holds that many men actively want their wives to take over their clothing problems just as their mothers had done. Consequently, copy for men's clothing should use words and ideas that are peculiarly effective on women. For instance, "the ensemble effect" shades, buttons, feel, and style.

Copy normally should state that "styling is new this year" (any year) and that exciting things are happening in men's fashions. Get across the idea that exciting things happen to men who dress in today's exciting fashions. Copy for the men's department of a department store should stress the location of the entrance to the men's store (or department). It usually is on the street. That implies that men don't have to traipse through displays of slips, bras, girdles and other intimate feminine finery before finding their own department. About 17 percent of this business is done in December, and about nine percent in each of the months of October and November. February is the low month, about six percent.

Helpful words and ideas

wearable	enjoyable	durability	wearability
durable		Masterful tailoring	
Rugged good looks		Smooth and powerful	
Rugged handsomeness		The powerful appearance	
The power fashions of today		A look of power	
Full, free, and impressive		The power of the NOW look	
Long-playing sportswear		The power fashions	
Masterfully tailored		At home anywhere	
Handsome ruggedness		Rugged durability	

ORGANS AND PIANOS

Motivation: Esteem, enjoyment, acquisitiveness

Key idea: Anyone can learn to play the organ.

There is music in everyone. The amount and the quality vary from person to person, but there is in everyone the capacity both to enjoy music and to produce music one way or another.

Overlaid on these basic facts is another: Most people believe sincerely that they cannot learn to play. That, perhaps, is the biggest obstacle to the sale of organs.

Most pianos are sold for the use of children who are learning to play. Organs are sold for all-family enjoyment and are as likely to be used by adult learners as by children.

Learning to play the organ is easier, faster, and far more satisfying to most people than learning to play the piano, because it is feasible to eliminate about two-thirds of the drudgery of scale practice. Most of the piano scale practice is for the purpose of strengthening finger muscles. The softer, sustained touch on the organ keyboard does not require as much finger strength. Consequently, the ability to play satisfactorily is achieved much faster.

Impressive organ sounds are produced by sustained keyboard pressure combined with volume controlled entirely by a foot pedal. While parents easily understand that enforced keyboard practice is good for the character of a child, they are inclined to look upon such repeated drills for themselves as an unnecessary waste of time. Organs, therefore, are far more attractive to adults for their own use than are pianos.

We are indebted to Joseph Bilotti, owner of Bilotti Organ Center, Trenton, N. J., for much of the insight into the pattern of organ and piano sales. It is far easier for an organ salesman to sell a $2,500 organ than to sell an $800 piano, he explained. An organ student of whatever age can be playing recognizable tunes, both right-hand melody and left-hand chords, in less than an hour.

While there is some variation according to geographical location, the typical organ-piano dealer does about 15 percent of his business in December. Business jumps from below the monthly average in August to about nine percent in September and escalates through December. In some areas, January is a good month; in others it's about average. March, July and August are likely to be your organ advertiser's lowest months.

You may find that his peak day for business is Monday, with Friday evening and Saturday morning following in that order. His peak week of the year is likely to be the week after Thanksgiving. Business booms from about 10 days before Christmas through the week after.

There is no significant coop money routinely available, but being of the same emotional, profit-conscious self-aggrandizing nature as everyone else, the holders of organ company purse strings sometimes can be sold on cooperating with individual dealer campaigns. The vision and the quality of your proposed campaign will have as much effect on that possibility as anything your station can do.

Helpful words and phrases

Learn to play

Play simple tunes in 20 minutes

It's fun to learn to play in a class of adults.

Fun and enjoyment for the entire family

Astonish your friends and neighbors

Magnificent walnut cabinet

Thousands of people just like you learned the thrill of playing by this same method last year.

Note: If John Caples hadn't beaten you to it, you could make history for your organ advertiser by beginning story copy with the line, "They laughed when I sat down to play." Despite its purely laugh value today, it was one of the most successful efforts in the history of advertising. Even though you can't afford to use that line, you can base your appeal on the same psychology of "it's easier than you think."

SUBDIVISION DEVELOPER

Motivation: For women, fulfillment

For men, refuge

Basic to both, happiness

Key idea: A wonderful place to live

The entire analysis presented under "Houses" applies to homes in a subdivision. A subdivision developed by one builder or a cooperating group of builders can reap tremendous profits from a well-planned radio campaign.

Most real-estate advertising is done in newspapers and is deadly dull, ignoring the basic motivating factors that influence people in selecting homes. Even when the builders or brokers go to big-space advertising and expensive 2-color brochures, their efforts usually are nothing but overblown classified listings with pictures.

A good copywriter can help the real estate sales organization create an image that distinguishes a particular subdivision from all other subdivisions in the market. They try to do that with a name. In a small market where Westlink is the only subdivision in town worthy of the name, it does have a distinction. But where eight to 50 subdivisions are scraping the barrel for names like Westgate, Rolling Acres, Rolling Hills, Harpeth Meadows, Fair Oaks, etc., the distinction is lost on home shoppers who see them all advertised in 2-column by five-inch spaces on the same page Saturday or Sunday.

A good radio campaign that builds an image of a subdivision as a wonderful place to live will do more for a developer than all the listings he can buy. When prospects decide that they want to live in his subdivision, they will stand in line to buy a house from him. The decision to be made is no longer: "which subdivision" but "which house in this subdivision"

It would appear to a casual observer that all houses or lots in a subdivision are sold routinely; most of them are, in fact. But the builder or the sales organization has thousands of dollars riding on the question, "Will we sell them all in one year or will it take three years"? If they can be sold in the minimum time, it increases the cash flow; he takes his profit, pays off his loan, and reinvests in another subdivision. If he can net $50,000 in one year instead of three years, then make another $50,000 the second year, a good image-building radio campaign costing him $3,000 to $12,000 a year is the best investment he can make in his selling effort.

Selecting an image to be created requires much thought, considerable research, and a minimum of discussion with the client. Use the business analysis form to get the information you need about his prospects. He is likely to be of little, if any, help in selecting an image. Chances are he is so close to the jungle of physical listings of bedrooms, kitchens, dens, bathrooms, heating systems and brick-to-grade that he can't see the trees of motivation growing from roots of emotional need.

It will be almost entirely up to you to show him how to relate his specifications to his prospect's emotional needs. Forget about physical specifications. Include a reference to

184

location, convenience, and quality, but concentrate on an image that can be defined in one or a very few words. It may be unwise to state the realistic definition in your copy. But you and your client should know and agree on what it is.

Maybe it's "where all the big operators live," or "the place for bright young men who almost have it made," or "just down the street and around the corner from the country club section," or "forward-looking young families live here for a few years before moving up to executive territory." You can think of at least two dozen more possibilities. List all you think might be appropriate. Cull them out, down to two or three. Weigh each of those two or three against the other. Consider how broad and narrow each may be. Decide on the one that most nearly includes your client's exact market.

For a subdivision that is well under way, a testimonial campaign consisting mostly of interviews with present homeowners already living there would be ideal. Interviews should, of course, be carefully directed and edited to make the points that build the image and eliminate those which don't.

For a new subdivision, production copy featuring dialogue between two men, two women, and a man and wife will bring out a well-rounded image, showing three somewhat different viewpoints of the subject. Scheduled in weekday drive times and-or weekend saturation, such a campaign could produce a miracle for your subdivision client.

THEATRES

Motivation: Happiness, enjoyment, sex

Key idea: Enjoyment of a memorable experience

Experience enjoyed in a theatre is 100 percent emotional, as far as the picture (or live production) is concerned. Drive-in theatres offer additional motivation. Families can take an evening out, dine on snacks from the concession stand, and Mom avoids cooking.

Transcribed material of the highest order of per-suasiveness is usually available. If not, certainly the manager has a press book, which contains proofs of all newspaper mats created for the picture as well as prewritten reviews. You can adapt that material to radio style and have better copy than you're likely to write otherwise.

Better yet is the technique of taking a recorder (with connecting lead and alligator clips) to the projection booth at an off-hour and dubbing the filmed promotion material to your tape. Then edit the tape to time and add your own lead, transitions, and closing. Many times you get the voices of the stars, as well as the emotion-charged voice of the production announcer. In smaller markets where theatre owners had been strictly newspaper advertisers and, therefore, extremely hard to sell, this technique has created loyal clients. It takes time, imagination, and a special effort. Whether you do it or not depends on management's desire for additional business. Note: See "Books," for techniques on selling emotional experiences.

TIRE RECAPPER

Motivation: Wealth plus complex automobile-related considerations

Key idea: Save money.

Check "Automobiles" and "Automotive Accessories" for a more complete listing of motivations. The thrust of the copy effort should be to convince prospects that it is smart thinking to use good recaps. A man who is proud of his car is likely to believe that his present tire bodies are good. He would be receptive to the idea of having them recapped in preference to buying recaps from stock. Since your client must also sell recaps from stock, do not make any such reference to stock. Use positive statements about the prospect's present tires.

It is worth noting that companies who take tires off a car, recap them, and re-install them in one day, are disappearing. More small recappers with that capability are going out of the recapping business than are entering it. Many are finding it more economical and otherwise satisfactory to buy recapped tires from larger "production" recappers who operate on an assembly line basis and serve recap retailers over a wide area.

While car fanciers are prone to make illogical decisions, they are quite receptive to a show of logic. Copy that gives down-to-earth reason-why proof, construction facts, and testimonials is recommended.

First, emotionalize, perhaps about good tires for a good car; a man who takes good care of a good car certainly wants to be sure he's running on good rubber, etc. Then, recaps are good, smart car owners know. Give reasons why, facts, proof, proof, proof.

Testimonials—perhaps a campaign built on one testimonial per spot—which say in effect that under normal driving conditions this specific set of tires ran a certain number of miles. The cost per thousand miles was this much. New tires would have cost this much per thousand for the same number of miles. In other words, a comparison of new tire and recap costs should motivate a prospect to buy the recaps.

Before writing copy it would be well to use the business analysis form to determine the facts about your client's prospects, especially income and age brackets, age of cars they drive, percentages of blue collar, white collar, women, teenagers, college students, etc. Persons who give testimonials should be selected to identify with the prospects. If a breakdown of tire prospects indicates that it would be suitable, a local high school or college star athlete would be good.

Other than well-known personalities, who usually are not practical choices at the local level, select a man who sounds like a typical prospect, someone who speaks with sufficient distinctness and does a type of work with which a large percentage of prospects can identify. It would be well to use testimonials representing several widely different types of people and employment.

TV SERVICE

Motivation: Happiness, enjoyment, wealth, family

Key idea: Fast, competent work at an honest price

There is a general distrust of TV repair service in two areas:

1. Faked or inflated costs

2. Intolerably slow service

Copy generally should be of an institutional nature to establish confidence and recognition when service is needed. It should be down-to-earth, and stress speed, without promising the impossible, and realistic rates. Ideal advertising is a continuing campaign planned for at least 13 weeks to educate and explain to listeners that:

A. Service call charges are realistic.

B. The temporary convenience of replacing a tube on a service call (without taking the set into the shop) can be offset by more extensive trouble and loss of service later.

C. The service policy and rates are realistic and work to the customer's advantage in the long run.

D. A TV set has **thousands** of trouble possibilities. Repairing one does not eliminate others.

Details to substantiate the above premises must be obtained from individual clients.

Helpful words and phrases

integrity	guarantee	enjoy
quality	fast	courteous
realistic		

Chapter 13

Sample Production Copy

In the first chapter we noted that "cartooning" can be effective only after you learn how to write undistorted copy effectively and according to basic principles. Successful "cartooning" or intentional distortion must come from a combination of a thorough understanding of the principles of advertising and your own personality. Stan Freeberg's work probably is the outstanding example of such success.

In the mid 60s three young Nashvillians, then operating as a production company for Nashville advertising agencies, expanded to agency status and specialized in unusual creativity that demanded attention. The partners, now older and ready for greener pastures, have gone their separate ways, but a representative sample of their radio copy lingers here for your analysis. The partners who produced this work were Paul Garrison, Travis Jones, and Larry Womack.

Remember, as you read the copy, that in radio advertising, as in face-to-face selling, enthusiasm is a key factor. Garrison, Jones and Womack wrote much of their own music and played it as well. They provided all the masculine voices, from the style of a straight announcer, standing on a pedestal, belting out the good word, to French, German, and British accents, old men, Brooklyn, and space men. Every line was rehearsed and analyzed for the most effective emphasis, attitude, and accent. Most lines were intentionally over-acted and emphasis was either exaggerated or underplayed. As Paul Garrison said, "When you get the adrenaline up and begin to jump around and wave your arms, you can get some good commercials."

As a staff copywriter you should realize that the total effort on the part of a conscientious director (who may be you) and capable talent can bring otherwise so-so copy to vibrant and effective life. By the same token, great production copy can be killed by the typical staff-announcer style of "selling."

Here are 27 examples of the Garrison, Jones, and Womack copy.

ANNCR:	(COLD) Now, here's Santa Claus for Nashville Motors.
SOUND:	CHRISTMAS MUSIC WITH BELLS UNDER
SANTA:	Ho ho ho. Now it's Christmas on Broadway and at Nashville Motors, so why not put a Buick under your Christmas tree. (SANTA THEN SINGS TO TUNE OF OLD FASHIONED FOUR-NOTE AUTO HORN) Mer-ry Christ-mas.
SOUND:	MUSIC UP AND SEGUE TO
GIRL:	(SINGING TO SAME TUNE OF OLD FASHIONED FOUR-NOTE AUTO HORN) Nash-ville Mo-tors.
SANTA:	Next to the railroad station on Broadway. Oh hohohoho Merry Buick, Merry Buick, Merry Buick (fading)

The next three, for Nashville Motors, featured the same girl's voice and ended with her own snickering laugh that is indescribable. Notice that the third sentence in each spot, "Opel Kadet?" has a questioning inflection. It was perfectly in character for the girl who had a definite but not exaggerated Southern "flavor" in her voice and for whom the copy was written. Probably it would be out of character in other regions.

OPEL:	(COLD) Hi there. I'm Opel. Opel Kadet? Like a combination of comfort, stamina and beauty for very little money? Then come see me at Nashville Motors. Who am I? Well, I'm Buick's new Opel Kadet, the lowest priced car made—by General Motors. Men who know me say I'm very easy to handle. And just look at my equipment that's standard. Full carpets, padded dash, a four-speed gear shift, and many more. Do me a favor. Come to Nashville Motors for a test drive. Just ask for Opel. (wild snicker)
OPEL:	(COLD) Hi there. I'm Opel. Opel Kadet? If you want me I can be reached at Nashville Motors. Who am I? Well, some call me a two-door sedan. To others I'm a four-door sedan or station wagon. Still, a lot of people call me a fast-back sport coupe. Really, though, I'm General Motors' lowest priced car. But don't let my low price fool you. Just look at some of my equipment that's standard. Bucket seats, seat belts front and back, padded dash, four on the floor and lots more. Do me a favor. Come to Nashville Motors for a test drive. Just ask for Opel. (wild snicker)

190

OPEL: (COLD) Hi there. I'm Opel. Opel Kadet? If you want me I can be reached at Nashville Motors, 242-5411. Got my number? In case you've forgotten, I'm Buick's new Opel Kadet, the lowest price car made— by General Motors. Why, the miles I can squeeze out of a gallon of gas will tickle you pink, and you should see my line. I've got five of 'em. I've got two 2-door sedans, a 4-door sedan, a station wagon, and a fastback sport coupe. See all of me at Nashville Motors. Just ask for Opel. (wild snicker)

Automatic Transmission Company, later Trabue Transmission Company, now Mr. Transmission, with franchises in nine states and plans to expand nationwide, doubled its business while this copy was running. The agency conducted a coordinated campaign using radio, billboards and newspaper. Some of the copy refers to other media.

SOUND: **SINGLE FRENCH HORN NOODLING A FEW NOTES**

FRENCH MAN: **NOODLING ALONG WITH HEAVY FRENCH ACCENT, FEW WORDS, ENDING WITH** Automatic Transmission Company.

ANNCR: Hey, hey, hey, hold it I dig the beat, but the French is a bit fractured.

FRENCH MAN: Oh, you refer to ze French horn.

ANNCR: No, the words, man.

FRENCH MAN: Oh, I simply say: If you have ze transmission trouble, go to ze Automatic Transmission Company. They're swingers!

ANNCR: You mean Automatic Transmission Company? The one with lifetime transmissions? Guaranteed for as long as you drive the car?

FRENCH MAN: Oui! Oui!

ANNCR: The one with free estimates on repairs, no money down, $10 a month, and seal jobs $25? Written guarantee?

FRENCH MAN: Oui! Oui!

ANNCR: Automatic Transmission Company, the Mid-South's oldest and largest? At 16th and Broad next to Jim Reed? And Murfreesboro Road near Warf Avenue?

FRENCH MAN: Oui! Oui!

ANNCR:	**We who?**
FRENCH MAN:	**Oh, oui! That is just an expression like "mo delawn."**
ANNCR:	**But what does that mean?**
FRENCH MAN:	**Mo delawn means "cut ze grass."**
ANNCR:	**Oh, pardon my French.**
SOUND:	**NEUTRAL BACKGROUND MUSIC UP AND UNDER**
ANNCR:	**(EXCITED) Say, that's not a French Horn. That's an automatic transmission.**
FRENCH MAN:	**Sacre bleu! You believe everything you read in ze newspaper?**

SOUND:	**BUBBLING WATER**
SUB:	**(THIS CHARACTER IS IN ECHO CHAMBER THROUGHOUT) Nuclear sub to Huntsville. Come in Huntsville.**

SNEAK MUSIC UNDER

ANNCR:	**This is Huntsville, heart of TVA and home of Automatic Transmission Company. (excited) What's that music with the bubbles?**
SUB:	**That's Lawrence Velk.**
ANNCR:	**You mean Lawrence Welk.**
SUB:	**You're right. Lawrence Velk.**
ANNCR:	**Thank you**
SUB:	**You're velcome. How's the traffic?**
ANNCR:	**A lot smoother, thanks to Automatic Transmission Company.**
SUB:	**(VERY FAST) No no no no ... I mean can I surface?**
ANNCR:	**Automatic Transmission Company goes way below the surface to find your transmission trouble.**
SUB:	**Just cover the vaterfront and let me know if I can ...**
ANNCR:	**Automatic Transmission Company doesn't try to cover the waterfront. They cover the one automobile**

	part that they know best. Automatic Transmissions. They'll repair or exchange any automatic transmission. Free estimates, no money down, $10 per month, seal jobs $25 and a written guarantee
SUB:	I am coming up now.
ANNCR:	Come up to Automatic Transmission Company, 403 Pratt Avenue North West.
SOUND:	BUBBLES
SUB:	Peace, O Huntsvillian.
ANNCR:	Peace, O Nuclear Sub Man. (EXCITED) Say, that's not a submarine. That's an automatic transmission.
SUB:	You believe everything you read in the newspaper?

SOUND:	HIGH-PITCHED SPACE WARBLING
SPACEMAN:	(IN ECHO CHAMBER THROUGHOUT) Space laboratory to Huntsville. Come in Huntsville.
ANNCR:	This is Huntsville, space capital of the universe and home of Automatic Transmission Company.
SPACEMAN:	(MAD NASAL LAUGH) He he he he
ANNCR:	What's the joke?
SPACEMAN:	I am ze mad scientist. I am supposed to go he he he he.
ANNCR:	What do you see from up there?
SPACEMAN:	Traffice jams. Everywhere traffic jams.
ANNCR:	Traffic's a lot smoother thanks to Automatic Transmission Company.
SPACEMAN:	I think I'll go back to ze star gazing. Or would you like to...
ANNCR:	Automatic Transmission Company does not stargaze. They focus on the one automobile part they know best. Automatic Transmissions. They'll repair or exchange any automatic transmission. One-day service. Free estimates, no money down, $10 per month, seal jobs $25 and a written guarantee. Automatic Transmission Company is located at 403 Pratt Avenue North West.
SPACEMAN	Come on up and take a look.
ANNCR	OK.

SOUND:	HOLLOW FOOTSTEPS RUNNING UP STAIRS.
SPACEMAN:	Peace, O Huntsvillian.
ANNCR:	Peace, O Mad Scientist. (EXCITED) That's not a telescope; that's an automatic transmission.
SPACEMAN:	HE he he he he. You believe everything you read in ze newspaper?

SOUND	DISTANT CANNON FIRING RAPIDLY.
GI	(IN ECHO CHAMBER THROUGHOUT) Artillery to Huntsville. Come in Huntsville.
ANNCR:	This is Huntsville, first capital of Alabama and home of the Automatic Transmission Company.
GI:	Artillery to Huntsville. Hold it a minute. Our cannon's jammed.
ANNCR:	Huntsville has a lot less traffic jams, thanks to Automatic Transmission Company.
GI:	Cannon's OK now. Give me the range.
ANNCR:	The folks at Automatic Transmission Company zero in on the one automobile part they know best. Automatic transmissions. They'll repair or exchange any automatic transmission.
GI:	(ANGRY AND IMPATIENT) Artillery to Huntsville. Will you please give us a target.
ANNCR:	Automatic Transmission Company. 403 Pratt Avenue, North West. One-Day service. Free estimates, no money down, $10 per month, seal jobs $25 and a written guarantee.
SOUND:	CANNON BOOM.
GI:	(SINGING QUIETLY AND SERENELY) I fly through the air with the greatest of ease. (END SINGING) Peace, O Huntsvillian.
ANNCR:	Peace, O Flying Cannoneer. (EXCITED) That wasn't a cannon you misfired. It was an automatic transmission.
GI:	You believe everything you read in the newspaper?

SOUND:	WEIRD SPACE SOUNDS

194

SPACEMAN: (IN ECHO CHAMBER THROUGHOUT) Space ship to Huntsville. Come in Huntsville.

ANNCR This is Huntsville, home of the Redstone Arsenal and Automatic Transmission Company.

SPACEMAN How's the parking problem down there.

ANNCR We don't have any problem with park...or drive...or reverse. Thanks to Automatic Transmission Company.

SPACEMAN But I'd like to explore the possibility of parking my space ship.

ANNCR: Automatic Transmission Company doesn't explore the unknown. They concentrate on the one automobile part they know best. Automatic transmissions. They'll repair or exchange any automatic transmission. Free estimates, one-day service, no money down, $10 per month, seal jobs $25 and a written guarantee.

SPACEMAN: Space ship to Huntsville. May I park?

ANNCR: Certainly. Come on down to Automatic Transmission Company, 403 Pratt Avenue, North West.

SOUND: RECORD STOPPED RAPIDLY ON TURNTABLE WITH WAILING SOUND.

SPACEMAN: Peace, O Huntsvillian.

ANNCR: Peace, O Spaceman. (EXCITED) Say, that's not a space ship. That's an automatic transmission.

SPACEMAN: You believe everything you read in the newspaper?

A series of 17 spots were written for Automatic Transmission Company, using the same format but substituting a different comic bit in each one. The jingle was the same at the beginning and end, consisting of original music and three well-emphasized words sung in a distinctive manner by Marti Brown, a local radio-TV singer who was a student at Vanderbilt University at the time. Trail music used only at the end of the spot was characterized by her distinctive and memorable "do do de do" type of sound.

SOUND: JINGLE

ANNCR: (DON ADAMS TYPE OF VOICE AND MANNER AS IF ON PHONE) That's right, a nationwide guarantee on all exchange transmissions. I certainly will. All right, who's next?

CHARACTER: You wanta hear my imitation of a car.

ANNCR: All right, let's hear it.

CHARACTER: (SOUNDS LIKE HORSE GALLOPING, TIGER GROWLING, AND SEAL BARKING)

ANNCR: That didn't sound like a car.

CHARACTER: Oh, yes it did. That was horses under the hood, a tiger in my tank, and a seal in my transmission.

ANNCR: You really know how to hurt a guy.

ANNCR: At Automatic Transmission Company, seal jobs are $25, just like it says in the newspaper. And they rebuild transmissions in their own Nashville factory. No money down. $10 a month. All exchange transmissions are guaranteed in 150 shops across the nation for as long as you drive the car.

SOUND: JINGLE

ANNCR: (OVER TRAIL MUSIC) 403 Pratt Avenue, North West.

SOUND: TRAIL MUSIC UP AND OUT.

COMIC BIT TO FIT INTO FORMAT.

ANNCR: (ALWAYS USING DON ADAMS TYPE VOICE) All right, back to the operation.

CHARACTER: Oh, doctor, doctor, doctor!

SOUND: RUNNING FOOTSTEPS.

ANNCR: Did you call me nurse?

CHARACTER: No, I called you Doctor!

ANNCR: You really know how to hurt a guy!

COMIC BIT TO FIT INTO FORMAT.

ANNCR: All right, who's next?

CHARACTER: Buddy...my transmission's slipping.

196

ANNCR: Well drive it up here on this rack.

SOUND: **FAST DRIVE UP AND SKID STOP (PRODUCED ORALLY)**

CHARACTER: How long you think it's gonna take?

ANNCR: Just one bit. All right men, ready?

SOUND: **REFEREE TYPE WHISTLE FOLLOWED BY FRANTIC SOUNDS OF METALLIC HAMMERING AND TAPPING.**

COMIC BIT TO FIT INTO FORMAT

ANNCR: All right, who's next? Oh, no. It's that seal again. Still working for the state, hah?

SEAL: No. I've got another seal job.

ANNCR: Really?

SEAL: Yes, I supervise a bunch of maids cleaning house.

ANNCR: What?

SEAL: I'm the good housekeeping seal of approval.

ANNCR: You really know how to hurt a guy.

Another Automatic Transmission Company copy series used testimonials. Purpose of the testimonial, which was part of an unrehearsed interview with a cross-section of the company's customers, was more to attract attention than serve as a motivating strategem. The motivation was provided by the announcer using standard copy, after the usually mush-mouthed interviewees had attracted attention by sounding different from the station announcer's polished and perfect diction.

SOUND: 500-CYCLE TONE (ABOUT TWO SECONDS)

ANNCR: Are you familiar with our advertising, sir?

CUSTOMER: Mmmmmmmm, yeah, I hear quite a bit of it on the radio.

ANNCR: Good, what'd you do about your car?

CUSTOMER: I guess that's one reason I called 'em. I heard it on radio.

197

ANNCR: Probably so.

CUSTOMER: They came out and got my car and they got...they got...you know...free wrecker service and all that...

ANNCR: Right.

CUSTOMER: ...and I went down there and they...they got working on my car pretty quick.

ANNCR: You have just heard a portion of an unrehearsed interview. This company is Automatic Transmission Company. Do not be confused by others who use similar names. Automatic Transmission Company offers free wrecker service, free transportation during repairs, one-day service on most repairs, and one hundred percent financing. Only Automatic Transmission Company offers a written guarantee on all exchange transmissions. Honored in 150 shops across the nation.

SOUND: **JINGLE**

Note: At the time most of this copy was running, a smaller company named Automatic Transmission Service was in business. Strong emphasis was placed on the word "Company" to distinguish the client as much as possible.

Here are transcriptions of six other interviews which were fitted to the same format:

ANNCR: Are you familiar with the advertising for Automatic Transmission Company?

CUSTOMER: Well...I've noticed a couple of billboards.

ANNCR: Have you ever heard the jingle?

CUSTOMER: No...yes! Yes I have.

ANNCR: Remember how it goes?

CUSTOMER: (TRYING TO SING) Yeah...it goes Automatic... les see... no it's Automatic Transmission Company.

ANNCR Yes.

CUSTOMER Yeah, I've heard it.

ANNCR: Thank you very much.

ANNCR Ever have any work done by Automatic Transmission Company?

CUSTOMER: (WOMAN) Yes I have.

ANNCR: What was the nature of that work, do you know?

CUSTOMER. My husband took my station wagon down there.

ANNCR: What was the trouble with your wagon?

CUSTOMER: Oh, ever' time I tried to go up a hill it felt as if my car wasn't gonna make it.

ANNCR: Are you satisfied with the car now?

CUSTOMER: Oh, yes, indeed.

ANNCR: Well...uh...how long ago did this happen?

CUSTOMER: Oh, 'bout three years ago.

ANNCR: Oh, really! Well, thank you very much

CUSTOMER: Well...I don't know too much about cars, but one day I was driving my husband's car and I had a little bit of trouble with the...uh...shifting of the gears. It was something...he said something slipped out of place. But he suggested I take it...I called...and he said take it...uh...

ANNCR: To Automatic Transmission Company?

CUSTOMER: To Automatic Transmission Company, and they fixed it and we haven't had any problems with it.

ANNCR: All right, thank you very much.

ANNCR: Have you ever had any work done at Automatic Transmission Company, sir?

MAN: No, I haven't. I don't even have a car.

ANNCR: Do you have any friends who have had any work done there?

MAN: Yes, I have. My buddy just took his car down there last month.

ANNCR: Really? What kind of work did he have done?

MAN: They did sump'n to the transmission or sump'n; it wasn't runnin' too good.

ANNCR: Well does it run fine, now?

MAN: Yeah!

CUSTOMER: Well my uncle very recently had his work done.

ANNCR: What kind of work did they do for him, do you know?

CUSTOMER: Uh...no, I'm sorry I don't.

ANNCR: Was he happy with the work they did for him?

MAN: Oh, yes. As a mattera fact he told me to stop by in case I ever had any trouble.

ANNCR: All right. OK, thank you very much.

ANNCR: Have you ever heard any of the advertising for Automatic Transmission Company?

BOY: I sure have. I hear it ever' mornin' on the way to school.

ANNCR: Would you remember any of it. Could you do any of it for us?

BOY: All I remember is that chick singin' that melody. (SINGING) Automatic foo fe doo fe doo doo doo.

ANNCR: (LAUGHING) Yes. All right, thank you very much.

---

1.   And now a word from Automatic Transmission Company.

2.   (WHISPERING) Automatic Transmission Company. Company?

1.   (ALSO WHISPERING) Yes. Company! There are others using similar names.

2.   Oh, I see.

1.   We're the Mid-South's oldest and largest automatic transmission specialists.

2.   I see.

1.   (BACK TO "PEDESTAL" STYLE DELIVERY) And now a word from Automatic Transmission Company.

2.   (CLEARS THROAT AND THEN USES STRONG BUT VERY LOW-KEY DELIVERY) For years we worked on just one automobile part, automatic transmissions. We worked hard. We learned more

about automatic transmissions than anybody in the Mid-South.

1.   So?

2.   And then the stick shift came back.

BYSTANDER:(IN DISGUSTED NON-PROFESSIONAL VOICE) Gee whiz!

2.   I'd like to say that we now repair stick shifts, three speeds, four on the floor, all makes and models. Also, we offer free estimates, no money down, $10 a month. At Automatic Transmission Company. 16th and Broad next to Jim Reed. And Murfreesboro Road near Warf Avenue.

BYSTANDER:Of course, you're still the Mid-South's largest specialist in automatic transmissions!

2.   (DEADPAN) Yes, and you can't beat that with a stick.

Here are three spots produced by Garrison, Jones and Womack for Hilltop Auto Salvage.

ANNCR: (IN SPORTS ANNCR STYLE) Hello there, sports fans. This is your on-the-scene sports reporter at the Cherokenapolis Speedway. We're about to interview the famous race car driver, Fireball Frenzley.

SOUND: ROARING RACE CAR GROWING LOUDER QUICKLY.

ANNCR: (EXCITED) Here comes Fireball, now.

SOUND: SCREECHING STOP

FIREBALL: (HE'S A DUM DUM WITH MORONIC STACCATO MANNER OF SPEECH) Hello there. I'm Fireball Frenzley, famous race car driver. How are you?

ANNCR: Yes. I'd like to ask how long have you been racing?

FIREBALL: What time is it?

ANNCR: Never mind. Do you feel that racing is getting safer or more dangerous?

FIREBALL: Yes, I do.

ANNCR: Well, have you had any interesting things happen to you, like a part falling off your car?

FIREBALL: Yes, I was in the big race one time and the parts fell off.

ANNCR: What did you do?

FIREBALL: I asked the garage man to go out to the Hilltop Auto Salvage, 2408 Dickerson Road, to pick me up an engine, a transmission, a front end, a rear end, three tires, and a battery.

ANNCR: Say, well, that's great; Hilltop does have reconditioned guaranteed auto and truck parts at one-half the cost of new replacement parts. By the way, how did the race come out?

FIREBALL: Well, by the time we got the things put on the car, the race had been over three days, huh...I will see ya, bye.

ANNCR: (LAUGH) If you need a good used auto or truck part, ask your garage man to get the part you need at Hilltop Auto Salvage 2408 Dickerson Road. Or drive out there yourself.

ANNCR: (COLD) Good morning, this is your on-the-scene reporter in downtown Nashville. We're about to interview the man in the street.

OLD MAN: Yeah, yeah, I'm the man in the street, and if I don't get out of it I'll be run over by a car.

ANNCR: It so happens that we're interested in cars. We ask people what they think of Hilltop Auto Salvage 2408 Dickerson Road. You are familiar with Hilltop?

OLD MAN: Friend, I don't get familiar with nobody.

ANNCR: Yes. Well, uh...Hilltop Auto Salvage has acres and acres of reconditioned guaranteed auto and truck parts, all at one-half the cost of new replacement parts.

OLD MAN: I once had experience along that line.

ANNCR: Well, just tell the folks about it.

OLD MAN: Well, one time I uz jest moseyin' down the road mindin' my own business, just goin' chug chug chug chug chug..."

ANNCR: All right! So what happened?

OLD MAN: Well, to make a long story short, out of a clear blue sky, KA BAM! Got busted in the rear end.

202

ANNCR:	And what did you do?
OLD MAN:	Well, asked my garage man to go out to Hilltop Auto Salvage, pick me up a rear end, transmission, carburetor, steering wheel, radio, three tires and a battery.
ANNCR:	Gee whiz, the other guy must have been going pretty fast. Did his brakes fail?
OLD MAN:	No, the other guy was parked. I uz drivin' in reverse at the time.
ANNCR:	(SMALL LAUGH) If you need a good used auto or truck part, ask your garage man to get the part you need at Hilltop Auto Salvage, 2408 Dickerson Road. Or drive out there yourself.

SOUND:	LOCOMOTIVE CHUGGING IN BACKGROUND
ANNCR:	Good morning. This is your on-the-scene reporter at Union Station. We're about to interview the famous railroad engineer, Casey Smith.
CASEY:	Hello out there in radioland. I'm the famous railroad engineer, Casey Smith, not to be confused with that other famous railroad engineer, Casey Brown.
ANNCR:	Yes, I'd like to ask, though, what is your opinion of Hilltop Auto Salvage?
CASEY:	(ATTITUDE OF INDIGNANT AND UTTER AMAZEMENT) Hilltop Auto Salvage?
ANNCR:	Hilltop Auto Salvage sells reconditioned guaranteed auto and truck parts at one-half the cost of new replacement parts. Engines, carburetors, front ends, rear ends. Ask your garage man to get the parts you need at Hilltop Auto Salvage, 2408 Dickerson Road. Or drive out there yourself.
CASEY:	(ANGRY) I'm against 'em.
ANNCR:	(SURPRISED QUESTIONING ATTITUDE) HMMM?
CASEY:	Frankly, I think Hilltop Auto Salvage is trying to put the railroads out of business. I mean you get a guaranteed truck part at one-half the cost of new replacement parts and you can afford to buy more trucks.
ANNCR:	So?
CASEY:	So we're getting enough trouble from the airplanes.

ANNCR:	Well, tell me, do you plan to put up a fight?
CASEY:	You mean fight Hilltop Auto Salvage, 2408 Dickerson Road?
ANNCR:	Yes.
CASEY:	(SLOWLY WITH DIGNITY) Us railroad men had rather switch than fight.
SOUND:	LOCOMOTIVE WHISTLE IN BACKGROUND.

The next series of copy, for Crescent Bowling Lanes, utilized a permanent format containing an attention-getter and an urge to action. Interest and (hopefully) desire were created by the comic inserts. One complete spot and three additional inserts are presented here.

ANNCR:	(POMPOUS DOCUMENTARY MANNER) Your neighborhood Crescent Bowling Lanes, with the South's finest bowling facilities, take you back
SOUND	DRAMATIC GONG SIMILAR TO CHINESE GONG WITH PULSATING VOLUME.
ANNCR	through the history of bowling.
SOUND:	SNEAK DRAMATIC MUSIC FULL OF FRENCH HORNS DENOTING MARCHING ARMY.
ANNCR	Here we are amidst the glory that was Rome. The Roman legions are marching back to the city from their brilliant campaign in Ethiopia... (ASIDE) Could I have some more mike cord. I'll try to get Julius Caesar over to the microphone. I say, Julius?
JULIUS	(OVERLY DIGNIFIED, LOW-KEY, LOW-TONE WITH SLIGHT BROOKLYN INFLECTION) Who'd you expect, Richard Burton? (IT COMES OUT 'BOITON')
ANNCR:	Yes! Well, no! I mean, uh...your legions have won a smashing victory in Ethiopia—just smashing. And what will they do now for relaxation?
JULIUS	Well, my Centurians will probably goof off at the bowling lanes.
ANNCR:	And, may I ask, what will you do?
JULIUS:	As you know, most of my spare time is occupied with war. I'll probably plan a few campaigns, a strike here, a strike there, you know, keep up an alley?

ANNCR: Yes, I know.

JULIUS: Then take my family to the bowling lanes.

ANNCR: You see, bowling has been the family sport for generations. Visit your neighborhood Crescent Bowling Lanes more often. Crescent Lanes are so modern, and convenient, and fun. There's hardly any excuse not to:

SOUND: BALL SMASHING INTO THE POCKET FOR A STRIKE.

COMIC INSERT

SOUND: SNEAK PATRIOTIC TYPE MUSIC

ANNCR: (TENSE DOCUMENTARY STYLE) The date: July 19th, 1588. The place: Plymouth Harbour in England. The next voice you hear will be that of Sir Francis Drake.

DRAKE: Hang the Spanish Armada. This bowling match must continue to its conclusion.

ENSIGN: But, Sir! The Spanish Armada is sailing by Cornwall now. They're coming up the English Channel.

DRAKE: Spare me, Ensign. They're right up our alley. We'll strike when we see the color of their pin—er, pennant. Shall we continue to bowl?

SOUND: WINDY STORM WITH ROAR OF THE SURF UP AND UNDER.

ENSIGN: (MUSING TO HIMSELF) Does look rather like rain. Perhaps a good rain will dash them against these rocks.

ANNCR: You see, bowling has been a favorite sport for generations.

SOUND: PATRIOTIC MUSIC UP AND UNDER

ANNCR: (TENSE DOCUMENTARY STYLE) The date: July 4, 1366. The place: London, England. The next voice you hear will be that of King Edward the Third.

KING (BLUSTERING SOUND) Hang it, Wembley. We've got to do away with that beastly sport of bowling. Our

205

entire military situation is going to pot. **Our archers are missing the target because they've been practicing with bowling balls rather than bows and arrows.**

SOUND: **SWISH OF ARROW THROUGH THE AIR.**

KING: **(EXCITED) Watch it, Wembley.**

WEMBLEY: **EXCLAMATION OF SUDDEN PAIN. HE'S BEEN HIT BY THE ARROW.**

KING: Wembley, it appears that you've been pierced by an arrow.

WEMBLEY: Yes, milord.

KING: I say, does it hurt, Wembley?

WEMBLEY: Only when I laugh, milord.

ANNCR: You see, bowling has been a favorite sport for generations.

The next comic insert was never aired because of a misunderstanding about Cleo's pet snake. It could have been saved by rephrasing.

SNEAK DRUM AND FLUTE MUSIC REMINISCENT OF EGYPTIAN ATMOSPHERE

ANNCR: **(WHISPERY STYLE BEFITTING THE LOCATION)** Here we are in Cleopatra's pad on the Nile. **(ASIDE)** Could I have some more mike cord, please. Uh...- Cleo?

CLEO: **(TALULLAH STYLE)** Yes, darling.

ANNCR: I've heard that bowling is your favorite pastime.

CLEO: Shall we barge over to my lane?

ANNCR: Yes!

SOUND: **DISTANT RUMBLE OF THREE BALLS STRIKING PINS IN SLOW SUCCESSION.**

ANNCR: You have nice looking pins. Are you good at it?

CLEO: Sometimes I miss the mark.

ANNCR: Those who bowl sometimes do. **(ASIDE)** Could I have some more mike cord, please.

CLEO:	Darling, that mike cord will be the death of you.
ANNCR:	Oh?
CLEO:	It's my asp!
ANNCR:	You see, bowling has been a favorite sport for generations.

Here's an example of odd-ball copy designed to solve a problem with which very few station copywriters are concerned. It, as well as the next eight, was written by Lou Nelson.

SOUND:	**SNARE DRUM UP UNDER AND OUT**
LOU:	Here's an excellent opportunity for a sharp, knowledgeable woman who can habla y scribe esponol y inglesa. If you couldn't translate that last sentence this job is not for you. But if you can take dictation in Spanish and English there's a tremendous job waiting for you now at Warner Lambert Pharmaceutical Company, Route 53, Morris Plains. This young lady will work in Warner Lambert's international division, where the duties will be secretarial in nature. There are many plusses with this job. Outside of a splendid salary with regular raise reviews, a 37-and-a-half hour work week, superior benefits along with excellent working conditions. This is a choice job and not everyone can fill it. But if you think you can, call the employment department today at 285-2892. That's 285-2892. Remember, the young woman we seek will be able to take dictation in Spanish and English and will work in the international division of Warner Lambert Pharmaceuticals, Route 53, Morris Plains, an equal opportunity employer. Don't wait to phone. Call now. 285-2892. 285-2892. Habla y scribe espanol y inglesa. Telephono dos ocho cinco dos ocho nuevo dos. Ole!
SOUND:	**MUSIC UP AND OUT.**

SOUND:	**DRAMATIC MUSIC INTRO UP AND UNDER**
LOU:	(TENSE DRAMATIC STYLE) The story you are about to hear is true, and took place recently at Schuler Tire and Service, Route 46, Dover. The customer's name will not be revealed unless you ask Ed Schuler personally.

SOUND: MUSIC UP TO PUNCTUATE AND UNDER.

LOU: A man walked into Schuler Tire and Service and said:

SOUND: DOOR OPENING AND CLOSING OVER MUSIC, WHICH CONTINUES THROUGH ENTIRE SPOT.

MAN: (HIGH PRECISE BOOKKEEPER TYPE VOICE) I bought this Golden Sonic 70 Polyester fiberglass belted tire from you people and your guarantee said that if something should happen to the tire, like a defect in workmanship, a road hazard, material failure, and I had less than half wear on the tire, I'd get a brand new one free, no red tape, no arguments, and no discussions.

LOU: Ed Schuler looked at the Golden Sonic 70 Polyester fiberglass belted tire, found that it had suffered a irreparable puncture and for safety's sake would not repair it. Ed Schuler found that this Golden Sonic had 7,000 miles wear, which was less than the half-way guarantee, and gave this man a brand new Golden Sonic 70 absolutely free in exchange for his tire. Not one penny changed hands, nor was there any red tape or any papers to fill out. The story you heard was true. It took place at Schuler Tire Service, Route 46, Dover. Remember, if it doesn't say Polyester fiberglass belted, it can't be a Golden Sonic 70.

SOUND: DRAMATIC MUSIC UP AND OUT.

SOUND: STINGER

LOU: Ed, where's James Bond now?

ED: He's on assignment in another part of the world.

LOU: Dana, we need help. Any suggestions?

DANA: Chief, we're number one in the plastics industry, right?

LOU: Yep.

DANA: There must be a way we can interest mechanically inclined persons to operate our type of equipment. And you must have an idea.

ED: Why not canvass door-to-door, telling people that Union Carbide needs competent intelligent personnel to work in the plastics industry and in return, since our newly announced pay increase went into effect, it'll mean good pay while you're learning.

208

LOU: I don't like the idea of a door-to-door canvass. Dana, any suggestions?

DANA: How about word-of-mouth, telling people to call the Union Carbide personnel office, 267-6000, for information and an interview appointment.

LOU: Ed, what are we specifically looking for?

ED: Chief, we're looking for production operators at Union Carbide. And it's a chance to get a head start on a career with a great company.

LOU: Dana, what's that personnel office number again?

DANA: 267-6000, and chief, the benefits offered at Union Carbide are really outstanding.

LOU: Then why do we need James Bond.

ED: He brings all those sexy dolls with him.

LOU: Ed, just what do you do at Union Carbide?

SOUND: MUSIC UP AND OUT

Note: In the preceding part, DANA is a part for a girl. She adds variety to the sound of two male voices.

LOU: (COLD) I'm Ray.

GIRL: I'm Bill.

LOU: You can't be Bill.

GIRL: Why can't I be Bill.

LOU: Bill's my partner. We're Ray and Bill, your American Motors dealer in East Hanover just across from Sandos.

GIRL: I say I'm Bill. You say you're Ray. How do I know you're really Ray?

LOU: Because I'm Ray. I've been Ray all my life. In fact Ray and Bill have been serving the community for over 22 years with the very finest in automobiles. Now, I should know Ray and Bill when I see them.

GIRL: Why, you mean when you see them. Let's get to the bottom of this. Ray and Bill are having a what?

LOU: An American Motors year-end celebration.

GIRL: That's right. And what kind of cars do Ray and Bill sell?

LOU: Ambassadors, Americans, Javelins and Rebels.

GIRL: Right again. And if you bought an Ambassador, would air-conditioning cost you more?

LOU: Absolutely not.

GIRL: So far, so good.

LOU: Thanks.

GIRL: During this American Motors year-end celebration, Ray and Bill have a slogan, "you could pay more..." Finish it.

LOU: "And get an ordinary car."

GIRL Excellent. What is Ray and Bill's phone number?

LOU: 887-5900.

GIRL And the location?

LOU: Route 10, East Hanover, opposite Sandos.

GIRL: I've come to a conclusion. You are Ray.

LOU: Gee, thanks, Bill. For a moment I didn't think you believed me.

SOUND: **LIGHT ROMANTIC MUSIC UP ONE SECOND AND UNDER.**

LOU: Joanie, before you go back to school, I'd like to give you this. Who knows, it may help you to get to school on time.

JOANIE: Oh Paul, this is a lovely watch. You really didn't have to, you know.

LOU: Why do girls always say that? I gave you this watch because I wanted to, not because I had to.

JOANIE: Paul, thank you for this gift. I'll treasure it. And it probably will help me get to school on time. Would I be too inquisitive if I asked where it came from? I love the way it's gift wrapped.

LOU: Well, quite frankly, it was kind of an impulse thing. I was on my way home when it started to rain like crazy. And there I was in the doorway of Marcus

	Jewelers in Morristown. **Rather than watch the rainfall I looked at their window display and then I saw it. The Omega you're wearing now. And I said "that's it." That's the perfect back-to-school gift for Joanie.**
JOANIE:	But it looks so expensive.
LOU:	Not really. **I opened a charge account at Marcus Jewelers, so in the long run everything is gonna work out just fine.**
JOANIE:	Oh, Paul, I'm so glad you bought it for me.
LOU:	Me, too. You know Joanie, I was just thinking.
JOANIE:	Yes?
LOU:	Marcus Jewelers, 45 Park Place, Morristown. They also sell rings.
JOANIE:	Ohhhhhh...
SOUND:	**MUSIC UP AND OUT**

LOU:	**(COLD; FAST INTENSE DELIVERY) Morristown Ford can't wait. We're overstocked with leftover 68s and they've gotta be moved.**
SOUND:	**DRUM RATTLE SIMILAR TO "MISSION IMPOSSIBLE" BACKGROUND UP AND OUT.**
LOU:	**Morristown Ford with two locations, 170 Madison Avenue, Morristown, and 240 Main Street, Madison, have over 300 thousand dollars worth of '70 Fords that must be moved to make room for the 71s.**
SOUND:	**HARD-DRIVING MUSIC DENOTING MOVEMENT OF ACTION, UP AND OUT.**
LOU:	**Morristown Ford isn't desperate, not yet anyway, but it's getting pretty close. So you come in today to Morristown Ford and pick up a model of your choice and take it for a test drive.**
SOUND:	**MUSIC UP AND OUT**
LOU:	**You've gotta be the winner with your '70 Ford from Morristown Ford. As for the price, man, we've slashed 'em to rock bottom. Now, these '70 Fords will move. There's no doubt about that. Morristown Ford is just anxious to put one in your garage right now. The 71s are coming and we want to be ready for them**

with the room they must have. So pick up your '70 Ford today from Morristown Ford.

SOUND: **MUSIC UP AND OUT (BARITONE SAX PUNCTUATION ABOUT ONE SECOND)**

LOU: It's a great car. We're great dealers. We back up our sales with service and satisfaction. Morristown Ford, 170 Madison Avenue, Morristown, and 240 Main Street, Madison. (PAUSE) A Morristown Ford is the smartest make you'll ever move.

SOUND: **LIGHT ROMANTIC MOOD MUSIC UP AND UNDER**

LOU: The whisper of autumn is in the wind, and soon fall will be upon the land and the bright scenes of spring will disappear. In its place will be a different, but also colorful season. Autumn has a mystery all its own. Why not be a part of it with a John Meyer Doeskin Philadelphia wrap coat from the Florine Shop, 13 South Street, Morristown. This John Meyer coat comes in several autumn colors and sizes eight through sixteen. When you walk in the Florine Shop and try on this Doeskin wrap coat you'll understand and be a part of autumn secrets. The Florine Shop has a unique way of making friends with the four seasons and they pass this friendship on to you in the latest styles, colors and fabrics. Remember, a John Meyer Doeskin Philadelphia wrap coat speaks your language. You can learn that language, the language of autumn, with just one visit to the Florine Shop, 13 South Street, Morristown. Use your Mastercharge or Unicard. The Florine Shop is open daily and Wednesday and Friday nights till nine. The whisper of autumn is in the wind and it's waiting for you now—at the Florine Shop.

SOUND: **MUSIC UP AND OUT.**

SOUND: **LIGHT ROMANTIC MOOD MUSIC UP AND UNDER**

GIRL: Sweetheart, I fell in love today.

MAN: I won't stand in your way. I hope you'll be very happy.

GIRL: I don't think you understand. I'm in love, hopelessly, desperately, madly in love. You know, of course, the problem this will present.

MAN: Yes, I don't know how the children will react to the news.

GIRL: It won't be too bad once they get used to the idea. I never thought it could happen to me. It started that

212

rainy Monday morning last week when I took your Maverick to Lou Miller Ford in Dover for servicing. You know, I had never driven your Maverick before, and when I got behind the wheel I had the strangest sensation and I knew right there I was in love.

MAN: Wait a minute. In love with what?

GIRL: With your Maverick.

MAN: (LOUDLY) Forget it. You can have the house, the bank books, even the one in Switzerland—but the Maverick is mine—forever!

SOUND: HAPPY MUSIC UP AND OUT

ANNCR: Don't let Lou Miller Ford, 200 S. Salem Street, in Dover, come between you and your loved ones. Get her a Maverick, too. She'll love you AND your Maverick.

SOUND: STINGER

LOU: (IN DRAGNET MONOTONE TYPE DELIVERY) One day a gunfighter, all dressed in black, rode into Dover. He stopped at one particular auto dealer and he called out:

GUN FIGHTER: (WHINNING NASAL SINGSONG VOICE) Lou Miller, I know you're in there Miller, and I'm callin' you out. Miller, you been selling those Fords, Galaxies, Mavericks and Mustangs at prices other dealers in this area can't match, Miller, and I've been hired to even up the matter. Other dealers know you can't be doin' business on the square, Miller, because you ain't makin' enough profit. They believe you've been auto rustlin' Miller, in the dead o'night—changin' colors, makes and models, an' then sellin' these cars at a much lower price. So I'm makin' my play, Miller. When this shootout is over there's only gonna be one man standin', so you had better get ready and plan to slap leather. 'Cause, Lou Miller, I ain't foolin.'

SOUND: MOOD MUSIC UP AND UNDER

LOU: (DRAGNET STYLE) Will Lou Miller strap on his guns or keep the vow he made when he was marshall of Skunk City. Join us again at this same time next week when you hear Lou Miller say:

MILLER: (UNCULTURED VOICE) OK, Black Bart, I hear ya.

SOUND: MOOD MUSIC UP TO CONCLUSION WITH ONE-STRING GUITAR RUN.

Note: A radio station staff copywriter for years, Lou Nelson has depended mostly on the station's over-the-counter record library for various sounds and types of musical production aids. Any imaginative and conscientious copywriter can do the same to good effect.

Here is some representative local copy used on Nashville stations in the first half of 1969.

SOUND: JINGLE (MUSIC ONLY OF WELL-KNOWN LOCAL STORE JINGLE. ELEVEN SECONDS TO ESTABLISH, THEN FADE AND HOLD UNDER)

ANNCR: The boy or girl graduate receiving a diploma this month deserves to receive a gift from Cain-Sloan. You may have been just guessing what the graduate wants, but Cain-Sloan knows what they want. Like the popular-sized 21-inch weekender luggage by Samsonite or American Tourister. Your choice only $35. Or Dominion hair dryer in luggage-type carrying case or Presto Shoe polisher set in wood-grain cabinet with foot-rest top. So don't guess what the graduate wants this year, give him what Cain-Sloan knows they want. And from Cain-Sloan congratulations to the 1969 graduate and sincere best wishes for your success and happiness. Cain-Sloan, Green Hills Village, is open tonight until nine.

SOUND: UP TO CONCLUSION. (WORDS OF JINGLE ARE "Cain-Sloan, Cain-Sloan, where selections are complete)

Written and produced at WENO, Madison, Tenn., a Nashville suburb, was this spot:

ANNCR: (COLD) You always get a better deal from Shelton Harrison Chevrolet in Ashland City. Here, now, is Mike Howell with more information.

MIKE: (TAPED AD LIB EFFECT) That's right, Chris. The 1969 pacesetter sale is in full swing. And Shelton Harrison Chevrolet in Ashland City sets the pace with the finest new and used car selection and prices. You'll find the fastest courteous service here at Shelton Harrison Chevrolet. If you don't believe me, come on in and check me out. That's what we want you to do.

ANNCR: Get the deal you want at the price you want to pay at Shelton Harrison Chevrolet in Ashland City.

This one ran on several Nashville stations.

ANNCR: (COLD) With all the mini dresses and mini glasses and other mini things nowadays, it's just natural that someone would come up with a (PAUSE ONE BEAT) Mini-Print. What's Mini-Print? Briefly speaking, it's a way to get your printing done in (PAUSE ONE BEAT) Mini-time. What's Mini-Print print? Well .... church bulletins, business forms, announcements, bulletins, catalog sheets, direct mail pieces, (DEEP BREATH) and if you need it, art work and typesetting as well. That's about it. But then again, what else is there? One other thing for sure. It's what you want but never get. It's a new printing service with a mini price. You've seen that yellow and orange bug shooting around town? That's Mini-Print delivering another job. Call them. Stahlman Building and 1808 West End building.

SOUND: (MECHANICAL SOUNDING VOICE MIXED WITH SYNCHRONIZED MULTILITH SAYING): Mini-Print Mini-Print Mini-Print Mini-Print . . . (AND FADE OUT)

On some stations the commercials are more entertaining than the programming. That may not be altogether true at WCTR, Chestertown, Md., but it might be if General Manager George F. Thoma (who has a staff of three and one-half in a town of 3,500) had more time to write.

SOUND: CROWD NOISE UNDER

ANNCR: Hello, this is your roving reporter at the Kent Plaza Shopping Center. I'm interviewing Christmas Shoppers today—finding out if today's shopper really knows what he's buying. I'm walking into Stenger Tru-Valu Gas and Hardware store. Oh, oh, there's a Christmas shopper.

SHOPPER: 140, 141, 142, 143, 144...

ANNCR: Excuse me, sir, may I ask what you're doing?

SHOPPER: Well, you see this 7-foot Scotch Pine Christmas tree? I've just finished counting the tips on this tree; and I find this tree has 144!

ANNCR: Is that good?

SHOPPER: Well, let's look at it this way. On my shopping trip I've found a similar tree with only 96 tips, but here at Stenger, this tree has 144 and costs only $18.88. That's a buy! Excuse me.

ANNCR: What're you doing now?

SHOPPER: I'm checking the prices on these aluminum trees—they've been reduced a third. For example, this 4½-foot aluminum tree is only $16.95.

ANNCR: I'm sure you really know what you're doing and buying!

SHOPPER: Do you see this 7½-foot Scotch Pine tree for $24.95?

ANNCR: You mean this one?

SHOPPER: Yes, this one. How many tips do you think there are on this tree?

ANNCR: Here, hold my mike, I'm curious to know. 1, 2, 3, 4...

SHOPPER: You're going to be here all night!

ANNCR: I'm started and I want to finish. 5, 6, 7, 8...

SHOPPER: There's 183.

ANNCR: How do you know?

SHOPPER: I already counted this tree. But you can check it. Stenger is open every night till Christmas.

Here's more of George's work:

SOUND: COCKTAIL COMBO UP TO ESTABLISH AND UNDER

ANNCR: Mother's Day is just around the corner. So for Mother's Day shopping make it easy on yourself. Shop eight specialty shops just for Mom, all in one convenient location—Leggett's Department Store in Kent Plaza Shopping Center in Chestertown, Maryland. Specialties for Mom include sportswear, lingerie, jewelry, cosmetics, shoes, piece goods, patterns, home furnishings, and housewares. Here's a Mother's Day gift suggestion from ....(insert name of store buyer)........

TAPE: (RUNS ABOUT 15 SECONDS)

ANNCR: Remember, Mom means a lot to us. So make that gift mean a lot to her. Make that gift a gift from Leggett's where you'll find eight specialty shops for Mom all in one convenient location. That's Leggett's—Kent and Queen Anne counties' largest and most complete department store in Kent Plaza Shopping Center in Chestertown.

At WBSC, Bennettsville, S. C., Harry W. Widdifield, who is something of a comic, writes copy and does air work under two different names. His approach to both copy and air work is quite relaxed and casual and his listeners think he's great. Here are two samples of his writing:

ANNCR: The guys in the big Detroit gas hogs used to say "bug" with a sneer when one came rolling down the street. Well, that was over ten years ago. And they still call it a "bug." But now they say it with respect. In fact, more and more of the Detroit hogs are being turned in for new Volkswagens. Why don't you get a formal introduction to the bug—or one of the new fastbacks, today, at West Volkswagen, Inc., U. S. Highway No. One, South, in Rockingham. You may not buy a Volkswagen, but you'll know you've driven a car for a change. See West today.

ANNCR: What to get Mother for Mother's Day? A new Ferrari! But if she's like my mother she'll complain about the gas mileage. How about a trip to Europe? Fine! But she'll spend the whole time worrying about whether or not she left the hall light on. Let's face it. What mothers want most for Mother's Day is something for their home. And Ushers Hardware is ready with Frigidaire matching washers and dryers and Frigidaire dishwashers. Perfect labor saving Mother's Day gifts! To give her more time to lay that new flower bed. Or paint the garage. For your mother for Mother's Day see Ushers, headquarters for the home. While you're there order your air conditioner ahead of the season and save. At Usher Hardware in Bennettsville. Beginning their thirty-second year of service to Bennettsville and Marlboro County.

At WHIN Gallatin, Tennessee, General Manager Charles W. Brewer writes most of the copy. Here's some of Charlie's work.

ANNCR: (COLD) Wiley Mobile Homes presents: The Cincher!

SOUND: DRAMATIC MUSIC INTRO

MAN: (PHONEY BUT DISTINCT FRENCH ACCENT) Ah, mon cherie je vu c'est beaucoup jene c'est pa—what to do! Kees me my darling.

SOUND: (EXAGGERATED KISSING SMACK)

MAN: Marry me, cherie, and I'll give you diamonds, expensive furs. Just marry me, mon cherie.

WOMAN: (PRACTICAL DOWN-TO-EARTH VOICE AND MANNER) Oh, Jaques, you're nice and you're rich, but...but...

MAN: My darling, I'll wine you and dine you in all the romantic capitals of the world. Marry me, mon cherie.

WOMAN: Oh, I do love you Jaques, and I will marry you if...if...

MAN: Name it, name it, mon cherie.

WOMAN: Jaques, all of those things are wonderful. But all I really want is my very own beautiful, comfortable, cozy Wiley Mobile Home. Jaques, I know we'd love living the life of Wiley.

MAN: Wow! Kees me mon cherie.

SOUND: SNEAK MUSIC

SOUND: EXAGGERATED KISSING SOUND.

SOUND: MUSIC UP AND UNDER:

ANNCR: Promise her anything, just be sure to include The Cincher, A Wiley Mobile Home. See Leon Kelley at the Wiley Mobile Home Sales Lot, Highway 109 South, on the lake.

Si Willing, president and general manager of KMAR, Winnsboro, La., and KNNN Friona, Tex., is one of the nation's truly brilliant small-market station managers. Among his many personal duties is that of writing much of the copy at KMAR. He reports that this copy, featuring the "Untouchables" theme, "drew a lot of customers. I had several rotating pieces of copy in the same idiom, but each featuring different items. The "Untouchables" theme hit me hard when I was groping for a new approach. It worked!"

SOUND: UNTOUCHABLES THEME UP AND UNDER

1st ANN: No other store can touch the low, low prices at Seligman's Department Store in Winnsboro.

2nd ANN: Blankets, all kinds of blankets on sale for one dollar each.

1st ANN: Seligman's untouchable low prices feature 100 percent cotton sheets and pillow cases for $1 each.

2nd ANN: Fifteen handkerchiefs for $1. This untouchable price is nothing to be sneezed at.

1st ANN   Compare anywhere and you'll find that no other store in this area can touch the low, low prices at Seligman's Department Store, Winnsboro, Louisiana.

2nd ANN: Listen for other untouchable low, low prices on choice merchandise at Seligman's Department Store, Winnsboro, Louisiana.

SOUND THEME UP AND OUT

Bob Moses, WKRM, Columbia, Tennessee, a student of The Power Technique Radio Copywriting course, made more progress toward professional copywriting ability than any other student. Here are three examples of his work on the Fifth Week's problems:

SOUND: (TWO RIFLE SHOTS)

ANNCR: To kill a Cobra snake may take two shots. But to get the best buy on a Ford Cobra only takes one if you see Chapman Ford. You can't miss at Chapman Ford in Donelson.

JEAN: Helen, have you ever had a Dior dress?

HELEN: Of course not.

JEAN: Well, I'm on my way to buy my first foreign-made dress. It might not be a Dior or even an original, but to be able to buy a bra shift in the colors and patterns that Belk's is selling during their Founders' Day sale will be something fabulous.

HELEN: I'm going with you 'cause as much summer weather as there is left, I could use a few summer dresses. And a swim suit—at Belk's low prices.

ANNCR: Go by Belk's today and get in on the many Founder's Day bargains. You, too, can save, save. That's Belks Department Store, Donelson Shopping Center.

SOUND: AUTOMOBILE RUNNING, UP AND UNDER

JANE: Oh, Honey, wasn't our wedding beautiful?

TOM: Perfect, sweetheart.

JANE: Oh, Tom, now won't you tell me where we're going on our honeymoon?

TOM: You said you wanted to go where you could swim and sun, didn't you?

JANE: Oh, yes, where the rooms were fully draped and carpeted in real elegance. And an ultra modern kitchen, in case I want to do a LITTLE cooking.

TOM: A convenient location where we could walk to the grocery.

JANE: And maybe a FEW outside activities, like a putting green. Oh, Tom, I know you found just the place. How long will our honeymoon last?

TOM Years, darling. It's our home at Robinwood Apartments.

ANNCR: Yes, you, too, can live the life of honeymooners at Robinwood Apartments in Hermitage Hills. One or two bedrooms, furnished or unfurnished, starting at $110 per month. That's Robinwood Apartments, 4830 Lebanon Road in Hermitage Hills. Go by today.

Mike Wyatt, who operates his own advertising agency in Trenton, N. J., wrote this clever copy series when he was on the staff of WBUD:

ANNCR Bob Drake, the man known as Delaware Valley's volume used car dealer, has done it again! He wasn't content with giving the best deals on used cars, he wanted to go all the way, and give everyone the best deal on used—and new cars! Bob Drake gets such a kick out of hearing people say as they drive away in a Drake buy, "We ALWAYS get a better BREAK from Bob DRAKE." So, he said to himself, "Self, why not make EVERYBODY happy. And give'em a better break on both used and new cars?" Now, to give the best break on a new car, Bob Drake figured he had to start with the best new car buy—and give a better deal on IT. He DID it. He went out to Wrightstown and took over Cherkos DODGE. It's now Bob Drake Dodge. A grand opening celebration is going on right now, and Bob Drake is giving deals never before heard of ANYWHERE. For a new or used car don't make a move till you take a gander at Drake. You always get a better break from Bob Drake. And it's better than ever before at the all new Bob Drake Dodge, Fort Dix and Charles Avenue, in Wrightstown!

ANNCR Bob Drake has a reputation of being Delaware Valley's VOLUME used car dealer. Why? Because he sells MORE used cars. WHY does he sell more used cars? Because you always get a better BREAK— from Bob Drake. However, not everyone WANTS a used car. Thousands of people have said to Bob Drake: "WE want a better break from Bob Drake on a NEW car." So I guess I'd better start with the new car that's the BEST buy. And give a BETTER BREAK on it! What NEW car is the best buy to start with? Right! The new DODGE! Bob Drake has taken over Cherkos Dodge in Wrightstown, changing the name, of course, to Bob Drake Dodge! He's making deals you can't resist! S'matter of fact, for a new OR used car, you shouldn't make a move till you take a gander at DRAKE! The all new Bob Drake Dodge, Fort Dix and Charles Avenue in Wrightstown, where a fantastic grand opening celebration is now going on!!!

ANNCR. Bob Drake, the man everybody calls Delaware Valley's volume used car dealer, has become one of the good guys. People have been saying that they always get the Best Break from Bob Drake. So, maybe we should say he's now become the "BEST" guy. He IS giving the "BEST" deals, on the BEST new car buy, the DODGE. Bob Drake has taken over Cherkos Dodge, changed the name to Bob Drake Dodge, and MAN, is he making DEALS! Bob Drake will now be known as the Delaware Valley's volume CAR dealer. New AND used! The all new Bob Drake Dodge is located in Wrightstown. You may drive a little farther to GET there, but you'll never drive a BETTER bargain! As Bob Drake, himself, says, "Travel a little and save a lot! Ask your neighbor, he'll tell you. "You ALWAYS get a better break from Bob Drake. And NOW Bob Drake offers you your choice of Dodges at a Bob Drake deal! Join in the grand opening celebration, NOW, at the all new Bob Drake Dodge, Fort Dix and Charles Avenue, in Wrightstown!

Here's spec copy Lou Nelson wrote when he was on the WBUD staff:

SOUND   HAMMERING

JOE   Hey, Fred, what are you doin? You look like you're havin' a fit.

FRED   Don't bother me now I'm teed off.

JOE   Don't get mad at me Fred, I just thought I'd lend you a hand; you look like you need it. What are you doin' anyway.

FRED   You know what I'm doin'; I'm puttin' up a TV antenna and you're right, I don't know what I'm doin'.

JOE   I know what you're goin' through; I almost tried to put up my TV antenna, but luckily my wife talked me out of it. She heard about Capital TV in Trenton; I called 'em up, told 'em I just bought a beautiful new color set, and I need an antenna installed. And would they come out and talk to me. Here's what Capital TV did for me. They put up this great colortron antenna, I don't know all the details about the low loss lead-in wire; that jazz is Greek to me. But the regular price is

221

$124.50. I got it from Capital TV, everything completely installed, for $79.95 with UHF-VHF and a 2-year written guarantee. Get smart. You could be up there all day. Here's Capital TV's number: 394-3550. They even got a Bordentown number. It's 298-2007.

FRED   I'm comin' down. Where's the phone?

Index